NOEL MERRILL WIEN
Born to Fly

An Autobiography

Foreword by
Major General Bill Anders
Chairman, Heritage Flight Museum
Apollo 8

ALASKA
NORTHWEST
BOOKS®

Library of Congress Cataloging-in-Publication Data
Names: Wien, Noel Merrill, 1930- author.
Title: Noel Merrill Wien, born to fly / Noel Merrill Wien.
Other titles: Born to fly
Description: Portland, Oregon : Alaska Northwest Books,
[2016] | Includes bibliographical references.
Identifiers: LCCN 2015041462 | ISBN 9781943328406 (pbk.)
ISBN 9781943328413 (e-book) ISBN 9781943328758 (hardcover)
Subjects: LCSH: Wien, Noel Merrill, 1930- | Air pilots—
United States—Biography. | Aeronautics—Alaska—History.
Classification: LCC TL540.W5133 A3 2016 | DDC 629.13092—dc23 LC
record available at http://lccn.loc.gov/2015041462

Front cover, left: This is Howard Wright's Hamilton Metalplane, the same model that my dad
flew in the 1929 historic first round-trip flight between North America and Asia. What a
thrill for me to have been able to fly it. Photo courtesy of Phil Makanna/Ghosts; center:
A recent photo of me wearing a cap with the Heritage Flight Museum's logo. Photo courtesy
of Phil Makanna/Ghosts; right: Me as a toddler in pilot gear. Back cover, left: Taken in Tokyo
while on a Genetrix mission, 1955; center: Wiley Post and Will Rogers arriving on the Chena
River near Fairbanks, 1935; right: Bill Anders on my left wing during a formation flight.
Photo © Lyle Jansma. Chapter opening airplane clip art © Rui Matos | Dreamstime.com

Edited by Janet Kimball
Designed by Vicki Knapton

Published by Alaska Northwest Books®
An imprint of

GRAPHIC ARTS
BOOKS®
Graphic Arts Books
P.O. Box 56118
Portland, Oregon 97238-6118
503-254-5591
www.graphicartsbooks.com

Contents

Foreword   5

Introduction   7

1. The Early Years 11
2. Young Pilot...22
3. Paid to Fly..40
4. In the Army Now 47
5. Aircraft Commander...59
6. Special Assignments 74
7. A Civilian Again 91
8. Alaskan Adventures... 102
9. Branching Out.. 116
10. A New Bush Plane... 137
11. Ice Island Flying 143
12. From the Turboprop to the Jet Age 153
13. Turbulence for Wien Air Alaska 160
14. Life After Wien Air Alaska 173
15. For the Love of Flying....................................... 183

Epilogue   197
Acknowledgments   204
Further Reading   205
Aircraft Flown by Noel Merrill Wien   206

Foreword

Imagine the surprise of an Air Force primary flight instructor when he finds out that one of his first students could land the aircraft better than he could on that student's very first flight. Imagine the young instructor's shock when he learns that his aviation cadet student, Merrill Wien, had over 1,500 hours flying time in various aircraft and was a qualified airline pilot in the twin engine Douglas DC-3 and the four engine Douglas DC-4, having flown for Wien Alaska Airlines and Pan American Airways prior to USAF service—and was also a certified Link Trainer operator! The USAF instructor's surprise was made possible because the ever humble "student," Merrill Wien, had not bragged about his background when he was initially processed into the Korean War–era US Air Force. Modesty is a Wien family trait.

I got to know Merrill when he joined our fledgling Heritage Flight Museum at Skagit Bayview Airport, north of Seattle. Because of his vast flying experience we made him our Director for Flight Safety and he flew our T-6 "Texan" US Army Air Corps trainer aircraft in formation with us at local air shows. Further, I had the honor of nominating the flying patriarch of the Wien family, Merrill's father, Noel Wien, into the National Aviation Hall of Fame, where he was inducted in 2010. The senior Wien's pioneering of Alaska bush and airline flying is legendary, but no more so than that of his son Merrill. Indeed, Noel's genes have produced several generations of fine aviators and flight attendants.

Noel Merrill Wien: Born to Fly is a great read for pilots, flight instructors, aviation buffs, and historians. It covers Alaskan bush flying and airline flying through the formation of Wien Alaska Airlines and subsequent leveraged buyout and liquidation. The Cold War found Merrill involved in little known covert flying in the very far north. Following military service, there was historic warbird flying and much more, as experienced through the logbook notes and vivid recollections of one of the finest pilots and nicest individuals I have had the pleasure to meet and fly with. Indeed, Merrill might have made a good fighter pilot except he just isn't cocky and braggadocio enough! Be it Piper Cubs on floats, Ford Tri-Motors on skies, helicopters, big commercial jets, or World War II B-29 and B-24 bombers, like *FIFI* and *Diamond Lil*, Merrill has flown them all and has interesting tales about many. His folksy and unaffected style makes his book a very enjoyable read and I highly recommend it.

BILL ANDERS
Major General USAFR (ret)
Chairman, Heritage Flight Museum
Apollo 8

Introduction

I never went looking for adventure but my early interest in flying brought adventure to me. Born into a family of aviators, I suppose I was somewhat destined to become a pilot. My father, Noel Wien, was one of the first pilots to fly in Alaska and his life was full of firsts, including making the first round-trip flight between Asia and North America in 1929.

My mother was not a pilot but she was notable in aviation in her own right, as she played a big role along with my father in the founding and development of Wien Alaska Airlines, the second-oldest scheduled airline in the United States and territories. My uncle Ralph, who died young in a tragic plane crash, was the namesake for the Ralph Wien Memorial Airport in Kotzebue and also contributed much to early aviation in Alaska. My uncle Sig, who eventually led Wien Airlines, was an automobile mechanic when he went north with my dad in December of 1930. He worked for the airline as a mechanic until 1937 when he got his commercial license. He then started flying for the airline out of Nome until my parents sold the airline to him in 1940.

So flying is in my blood and though my father never encouraged me to become a pilot, it was all I wanted to do from a very young age.

Except for the early years when I was building time for additional ratings, I didn't keep a logbook again for quite a while until I was required to as a Federal Aviation Administration (FAA) examiner. I cannot tell you how many hours I have to the nearest 10,000 hours. My father kept a very accurate logbook with comments about each flight but I could not imagine that I was doing any flying that would ever be noteworthy, since in my view all the historical and interesting flying had already happened. But as the years have passed, I've come to realize that I've been part of something that might be interesting to pilots, and others, today. I've told my sons: log your flying time with comments about each flight. I sure wish I had. Aviation keeps advancing so today's doings will be history tomorrow.

There is a lot to be said about the "good old days." Some of my fondest memories are from the piston engine days when I was scheduled to depart Fairbanks on a cargo flight about 3:00 A.M. on a midsummer day with not a cloud in the sky or a breath of wind. The still in the air is almost deafening. Your senses take on a very different perspective when there is not a sound to be heard except for some occasional birds.

I always felt that I was overpaid because I loved to fly. If I had had other income I would have paid to have the opportunity to fly. Even though this perhaps was less true in the later years when much of the flying was delegated to computers and flying talent was more about computer pro-gramming than seat of the pants flying, I still thought it was a great job. I feel very lucky to have had an occupation that I looked forward to every day. It was also an excellent opportunity to see many parts of the world that otherwise I would not have seen.

Part of the joy of flight for me and pilots like me comes from trying to master the airplane and complete a perfectly executed flight, an all but impos-sible challenge that consumes those of us who are passionate about flying. We can come close but I guess it is like golf. No one has been able to complete a whole game with every shot a hole in one but people are still addicted to golf like I am to airplanes, always trying to get close to the perfect game.

I think more people would travel by air if they realized that it is so much safer to take the airline than go by car. I am basically scared of heights but it is different in an airplane. I can't really explain why except to say that in an airplane I feel safely enclosed but in other high places it feels like it is just a matter of one false step.

I am a person whose mind has been in the clouds most of my life, star-ing out the window of study hall as a high school student, hoping to see an airplane fly by on final approach to landing at Weeks Field in Fairbanks, Alaska. I can't tell you why I have always been drawn to flight any more than I can tell you why the ancient mariners were attracted to the sea and the ships. I am reminded of the poem *Sea-Fever* by John Masefield, "I must go down to the seas again, to the lonely sea and the sky. . . ." I guess the explanation would be that at some point in time, I came down with sky fever.

My dad very often brought back toy airplanes made by Alaska Natives in the outlying villages.

The Early Years

In May 1930, there was a picture of my mother and me on the front page of the Minneapolis-St. Paul newspaper, stating that baby Noel Merrill Wien "lays claim to having the most flying time of any 'aviator' his age in the United States." I was eleven weeks old and, lying in a wicker clothes basket, had been flying in a 1930 Stinson with my mother and dad all over the Midwest, visiting air shows and airplane manufacturers. I suspect that my interest in aviation began at that early age, probably through a vibration osmosis from the plane, which my dad had recently purchased to take back to Fairbanks, Alaska, where we lived.

My father was already well known by this time because of his exploits flying in Alaska and his visit to Minnesota, the state where he grew up, was big news. When he arrived in Alaska in 1924, there were few airplanes flying there. Since that time, he had completed the first airplane flight between Anchorage and Fairbanks, the first round-trip in an airplane between North America and Asia, and the first one-way flight between Asia and North America. He also made the first flight north of the Arctic Circle anywhere in the world, as well as many other first flights within Alaska. He did not know he was making history at the time. He just loved to fly and was determined to make a living at it.

My younger brother, Richard, and my younger sister, Jean, and I were not really aware of my father's fame when we were growing up. He was just fun to be with and he seemed to be well liked by everyone around us.

I loved hearing about the flying experiences of other pilots we encountered in our daily life. My dad did not talk much about his experiences unless he was asked a specific question.

When I was about five years old, I remember asking my mother, "Am I ever going to grow up?" She said, "All too soon." I have thought about that day, which seems a very short time ago, many times. I was in a hurry to grow up because I was living among airplanes and pilots and I wanted to be a part of that exciting world. I could not wait to get my hands on the controls.

I always looked forward to Dad returning after he was gone for several days because he quite often brought me a present, usually an airplane that the Natives from the outlying villages had carved. I never expected a present other than a toy airplane. I made my first model airplanes out of toothpicks and tissue paper. Eventually, an older friend in the neighborhood, Frank Conway, was kind enough to teach me to build with model airplane kits and to show me how to fly them. In those days, the power models flew "free flight," meaning they were trimmed to climb making left turns with the help of engine torque and when the engine quit, they would descend in right turns minus torque and hopefully land not too far away.

Later, I got into control line flying. The ignition on the gas engines operated with two flashlight batteries, a coil, and a condenser, which provided spark plug ignition through points that opened and closed on a cam on the crankshaft. When the engine would not start it was usually due to no spark. When this happened, I often persuaded Richard to put his hand on the spark plug to see if there was any spark. When he resisted, I told him that if he didn't do it, he could not watch me fly. He finally figured out that I had no way of preventing him from watching. As he got older, he blamed his hair loss on all of the electric shocks I forced on him.

One of the best things about airplane-crazy kids having a pilot for a dad is that we ended up with old airplanes in our backyard that provided endless hours of fun and fed our dreams about someday becoming pilots. The first old plane was an Avro Avian biplane that my dad's good friend Robert Crawford had crashed. Somehow my dad ended up with it and even though he had the Wien mechanics rebuild it, he never trusted the splices in the fuselage enough to fly it. So Richard and I got it.

Then when I was around twelve years old, my brother and I talked the owner of a Kinner Bird biplane into selling it. It had been sitting at Weeks Field for years and was complete except for the engine. We paid five dollars of our hard-earned allowance money for it. What a find that would be today. As I remember, the wings had been removed and were lying alongside the airplane. We didn't even bother to take them with us. As we walked home pushing the fuselage, a policeman stopped us and asked where did we think we were going with that airplane? We had to stay there until he verified the transaction from the seller. That Kinner powered Bird provided us with many good hours of simulated flight, but in time we decided to remove the fabric and cover the bare fuselage with canvas and make a boat out of it. We lived near a slough and longed to get out on the water. That plan didn't turn out too well. But, always full of new ideas, I decided I would convert the fuselage into a helicopter using the old Avro engine that was stored in the Wien hangar. After I finished drawing up my plans for the helicopter, I showed them to my dad. He acted very impressed and told me that he thought it would fly. Encouraged by his comments, I went to work but eventually I ran into structural and design problems and aborted the program due to lack of funding. My twenty-five cents a week fell short on costs. I sure wish I had that rare airplane now. . . .

As I grew older, it didn't take me long to figure out that the gasoline engine could open up a whole new world for me. In the back of the Pacific Alaska hangar, there was a dump where they discarded old airplane parts and my friends and I would scrounge through it looking for construction material. One day we discovered a motorcycle frame with an engine still attached. We unbolted the engine and dragged it home in a little wagon.

Inside a tent in the backyard, I was busy dreaming up plans for how to use the engine when a stranger appeared at the tent opening. He was searching the neighborhood for his missing engine and was giving me a good chewing out when my mother heard the commotion and came out of the house. She did not like seeing her son being verbally abused and gave the man a tongue lashing in the way only a mother could do. He took the engine back, but a few days later I found a small 5/8 hp engine sitting on the front steps. I guess the man took pity on me and saw that I was simply a curious kid. It did not have much power but it was self-contained with the fuel tank in the frame and it ran perfectly.

Anything motorized caught my attention. A close family friend, Joe Crosson, built a small go-cart for his sons with a Maytag gas-powered washing machine engine. It was a masterpiece of engineering. Day after day, Joe allowed me to share it with his sons on the Pacific Alaska Airways ramp at Weeks Field, giving me a thrill that I was able to drive a "car."

I figured out another way to benefit from motorized transportation. When I knew that my father was due home from the airport, I waited for him with my bike at the corner of our block and intercepted him on the road. He would slow down and let me put my right foot on the running board of our 1941 Studebaker while I hung on to the door sill with my right hand, steering the bike with my left. That was the only way I could figure how to motorize my bicycle. Sometimes he would go around the block to give me an extended ride.

As I grew into my early teens, my father let me drive the Wien Airlines tractor that they used to tow airplanes. When we used it to landscape our yard, my younger brother and sister would hang on to the drag as I towed it and it was great fun. In later years when I worked for Wien Airlines after school and on weekends, they let me tow airplanes with that tractor. It was all part of my learning and I'm sure my early interest in all things motorized helped me when I began learning to fly.

In the years that followed, I yearned for motorized transportation of my own. I finally determined that if I were ever going to have a car, I had to build it myself. I scrounged airplane parts from the Wien hangar—wheels, tail wheel forks, steering wheels, and tubing—and talked the mechanics into welding the different parts together. For the pulley that I needed to mount on the drive wheel I bolted two pizza pans together. I scrounged a V belt from an old car and installed the 5/8 hp engine that had been given to me. I guess you would call the transmission a direct drive system. I built about three go-carts and they all ran, if only for a short distance.

MY FASCINATION WITH AIRPLANES CAME NOT ONLY FROM having a well-known aviator as my father, but also from my exposure to the pilots and flights that passed through Fairbanks, an aviation crossroads at that time, throughout my childhood. When world renowned pilots and airplanes would arrive in Fairbanks, most of the town, including my family, went to the airport. It was an educational experience for me to see these different airplanes and hear about their missions.

When I was about eight years old, I remember meeting Robert Crawford, the composer of the Army Air Corps song, and sitting on the floor next to the piano, watching him bang out "Off We Go" so loudly that I had to cover my ears.

The first Army airplanes—two Douglas O-38 biplanes—arrived at Weeks Field in 1934 to survey Alaska for an Army airfield location. President Roosevelt was concerned that Alaska might be vulnerable to attack, but this was still a time when the Navy's viewpoint about national security held sway; battleships were considered more important than air power. For years, General Billy Mitchell had tried to convince the military that airplanes were critical to national defense and he made this point so strongly that he was later court-martialed for insubordination. In 1925, he had even forecast that someday the Japanese would attack Pearl Harbor from the air, and this, of course, is exactly what happened. The Japanese paid attention to General Mitchell and so at the beginning of World War II, they had more airplanes and aircraft carriers than the United States. It's too bad we didn't listen to him. Shortly after the O-38s, Major Hap Arnold arrived with ten Martin B-10s to prove the capability of the Air Service as they continued to push for more emphasis on air power.

In 1935, I was playing with my friend Earle Grandison, and we saw Wiley Post and Will Rogers flying over Fairbanks. Their plane was a Lockheed on floats, which was actually assembled from parts of two different Lockheeds. Wiley had installed a larger engine with a heavier than usual three-bladed propeller, making the plane very nose heavy. It probably never should have been certified. I accompanied my parents to watch their arrival on the Chena River, right about where Ladd Field (now Fort Wainwright) was later built. This was just a few days before Post and Rogers were killed when their plane crashed near Point Barrow. My father ended up getting involved in this piece of history as he made a historic flight, racing against another pilot, to deliver the first photographs of the crash to the news outlets in Seattle. After flying all night, my father got to Seattle first, beating the other pilot by two hours.

Howard Hughes arrived in Fairbanks in 1938 on his record-setting flight around the world. At the time, his stop in Fairbanks did not have much significance for me other than the fact that I was impressed by his big, beautiful airplane. But now when I look back at the memory, I realize that I witnessed a historic flight by a famous pilot. I then remember some Japanese pilots arriving in 1937 in a Mitsubishi G3M bomber, supposedly on a goodwill trip. I heard a bystander say that they were probably there to survey Alaska. It didn't mean anything to me then, but it's funny how you remember these things years later.

My parents never encouraged me to be a pilot. I suppose my dad recognized that my enthusiasm was obvious. I don't think my mother wanted me to be a pilot but she never discouraged me. She had lived through times when my dad had been overdue for weeks and she hadn't known if she would ever see him again.

I was so fortunate to have been able to experience the thrill of flight at an early age. Though I preferred to fly with my dad, I jumped at the chance to fly with anyone who would take me. But I remember coming home, excited to tell my dad about a great flight I had with someone else, only to be scolded about flying with someone he didn't know. Not everyone was as safety conscious as he was and he wanted to be sure I flew only with people whose flying abilities he trusted.

When people talk about the good old days, believe me, they really were the good old days. I have owned many different airplanes during my lifetime but as the years passed I began to look back at the airplanes of the 1920s and 1930s with a great deal of nostalgia, partly because those were the airplanes my dad made history with. Newer airplanes were more efficient in speed and comfort but I would love to have been able to fly more of the planes my dad flew. The early Stinsons, Travel Airs, and Fairchilds seem to have a personality that is not found in modern airplanes and I will never forget the distinct vibration and sound of those old planes, and the way they smelled of adventure and excitement.

I vividly remember riding with my dad in the Fairchild 71, Travel Air 6000, or Cessna Airmaster on floats as we departed Fairbanks on the Chena River, which runs through downtown. At that time, the Chena was the only waterway near Fairbanks for float operations but it was a fairly dicey takeoff location. People would gather on the riverbank when they heard the engines start. It was impressive to watch.

Before starting our takeoff, my dad would taxi upriver to the usual starting point under the Cushman Street bridge. After he turned the plane around and throttled up for the takeoff, it always looked like the propeller was going to hit the bridge as the nose came up before getting on the step (planing on the water). Then it would look like we were not going to make the first turn in the river, which was quite sharp. I always thought the left wing was going to hit the high bank by the Northern Commercial company store during the right turn before reaching the straightaway for the anticipated liftoff. Sometimes if we had a heavy load in the plane, my dad would have to make one more sharp turn to the left on the water. This was always a terrifying experience for me but I never turned down the opportunity. I think it was a safe operation because most pilots knew their airplane's performance capabilities and they were confident in their abilities, but it was still scary when you were sitting in the cabin during takeoff.

When I was about ten years old I thought I had my big chance to fly an airplane. I had flown with my dad in the Tri-Motor Ford many times but seldom in the cockpit. Usually, my uncle Fritz rode along to function as a mechanic and to help with the loads so I was relegated to a cabin seat. This time, my dad was doing a test hop without Fritz so I happily climbed into the cockpit's right seat.

The Tri-Motor's brakes were controlled by a gearshift-type lever between the seats, commonly called a Johnson bar. Pulling the lever straight back applied the brakes to both wheels; moving it to the left or right provided differential braking. Because the brakes were not on the rudder pedals, a pilot needed three hands to control throttles, brakes, and control wheel. So the technique was to use the right hand for the brakes for ground steering and the left hand for the throttles on takeoff until directional control was available with the rudders. When I saw that the control wheel was unattended, I was certain that this was my chance to do the takeoff so I grabbed the wheel. Everything was going fine until the rudders became effective, whereupon my dad transferred his left hand to the wheel and the right hand to the throttles. Then it was time to raise the tail; when he pushed the control wheel forward, it was pulled out of my hands, but not without some effort since I had a firm grip on it. I then realized that I was not going to get checked out in the Ford that day. The fact that I could not reach the rudder pedals did not concern me; they looked like footrests to me.

Somewhere around the early 1940s, I had the opportunity to fly to Anchorage with my dad in a Travel Air 6000A. He had purchased a set of floats from Bob Reeve, founder of Reeve Aleutian Airways, and was taking the Wien chief mechanic, Ernie Hubbard, to install the floats on the plane in Anchorage. Airplanes were still somewhat of a rarity in Alaska at that time so when we arrived, there were only two floatplanes on Lake Spenard—one belonged to Bob Reeve and the other belonged to Art Woodley, founder of Woodley Airways, which later became Pacific Northern Airlines. (Many years later I was driving with my dad in the area and we saw hundreds of floatplanes parked side-by-side all around Lake Spenard and neighboring Lake Hood. Hundreds more were parked on wheels on land. He said, "Never in my wildest dreams would I ever have thought that I would see this many airplanes here.")

Spenard Lake was linked to Lake Hood by a recently built canal. Both lakes were limited in size and the new canal provided a longer takeoff area, enabling airplanes to take off with heavier loads. We landed alongside the canal on a new landing strip. Ernie installed the floats on the plane and then it was hoisted into the canal and we prepared for takeoff. Try as he might, my dad could not get the Travel Air on the step; he just didn't have enough power. Bob Reeve offered to lend him a longer propeller, more suitable for float operations. That did the trick and we were on our way to Fairbanks. I remember that my dad had to work the rudders all the way to Fairbanks because the floats caused quite a bit of instability around the yaw axis. After arriving in Fairbanks, Ernie added a fixed rudder under the rear of the fuselage, which was a big help. On each one of these trips with my dad, I watched him handle the controls, saw the results, and learned a little bit more.

When I was around twelve years old, I was convinced that I had it all figured out and longed for the chance to fly. My dad rented a Piper J-3 Cub at Weeks Field in Fairbanks and this became my first opportunity to do a takeoff in an airplane. I was anxious to demonstrate my flying ability to my dad as he sat behind me. I managed to get it into the air, probably with some help that I was not aware of. I flew around for a while and then it came time to make a landing. I managed to get lined up with the runway and thought this would be the easy part; however, the ground came up much faster than I expected and it was a jarring experience. The airplane was fine but my confidence was severely damaged. I learned then that my dad's approach to teaching was to sit quietly and do nothing to help me unless he thought that intervention was needed to avoid bending the airplane. One time when I was about fifteen years old, we rented a surplus Boeing Stearman at Paine Field in Everett, Washington. I thought my takeoff was going well until I felt the rudder pedals moving rapidly to avert a ground loop. I had no idea that I was about to lose control.

My experience in the Piper Cub set my confidence back for a while and gave me a lot to think about, but it didn't affect my desire to learn to fly. I wanted to be a pilot like my father. His fame as an aviation pioneer was well recognized but for me and Richard, his talents as a father dominated our admiration. He always tried to help me achieve my dreams, whatever they were. I was immensely fortunate, also, to have my younger brother, Richard, who was as anxious as I was to follow in our father's footsteps. We shared our love of flying throughout our lives. In addition to being an exceptional pilot, Richard's vision and analytical talent have always amazed me.

FLYING IN ALASKA WAS ALWAYS A DANGEROUS AND difficult business. My father had left Alaska in the fall of 1924 because winter operations were not possible with the airplanes available at that time. When he returned for the summer season in 1925, he brought his brother Ralph with him. He taught Ralph to fly and they worked closely together for the next several years. In 1929, Ben Eielson, a pilot who had gained fame when he flew Sir Hubert Wilkins across the Arctic from Point Barrow to Spitsbergen, Norway, offered to buy Wien Alaska Airways. He represented a company that planned to create an air transportation system throughout Alaska. My father saw a chance to explore other opportunities so he accepted the offer and he and my mother headed for Minnesota for my birth. En route to Minnesota, they heard that my father's dear friend and fellow Alaskan pilot Russell Merrill, for whom I am named, had disappeared flying out of Anchorage. Not long after that, Ben Eielson died when his plane crashed on a flight to Siberia. This was in the same Hamilton airplane that my dad flew on a similar mission earlier in the spring to retrieve furs from a different icebound vessel. Then an even bigger blow: While in Minnesota, they received word that his brother Ralph had died in a crash of an experimental diesel-powered Bellanca in Kotzebue.

When we returned to Fairbanks, my father's younger brother, Sig, came with us. Sig and my dad flew home in my dad's new Stinson while my mother and I took the train to Seattle, the Alaska Steamship to Seward, and then the train to Fairbanks.

My uncle Sig learned to fly in Alaska. He built up his time for his commercial license in a Buhl "Bull" Pup, which was powered by a three-cylinder Szekely engine of 45 hp. He became known for his pioneering flights in the Alaskan Arctic and was revered by the Native people there for his dependability, work ethic, and the services he provided to them. He was responsible for convincing the nomadic Eskimos who followed the caribou herds for food on the North Slope to settle in Anaktuvuk Pass so he could better serve them and keep them supplied. Some Native babies were even named Sigwien, as the people there had always treated his name as one word.

During the 1930s my dad worked to build his new company, Wien Alaska Airlines. By 1936, he had three other pilots and five airplanes: a Bellanca CH300, a 1933 Stinson, a 5AT Ford Tri-Motor, a Fokker Universal, and a Cessna C-34 Airmaster. By that time there was a lot of competition and it had become a cutthroat business to be in. It also was very hard to keep pilots. As soon as they gained experience, they would quit and start their own airline, creating more competition. In the late 1930s Wien Alaska Airlines lost five pilots in crashes. Those were tough times, yet my parents persevered.

In the early 1940s, my mother became very ill. The hospital bills drained my parents' resources so they sold the airline to my uncle Sig to help pay expenses. All the airplanes were paid for and in good shape and my parents were proud of what they had been able to accomplish through sacrifice and hard work. Eventually my mother recovered but my dad grew less and less involved with the airline over time. He continued as a pilot for a time and was on the board of directors until he passed away in 1977, but he was no longer involved in the day-to-day management. After Sig took over, the management philosophy changed. Sig spent most of his time flying in the northern part of Alaska; however, the airline continued to grow because my father was loved throughout Alaska and the airline remained associated with his good reputation. Even though my parents sold it, the airline that my father started was destined to be a big part of my life.

On the morning of December 7, 1941, the phone rang. I could tell that it was something serious by the look on my dad's face. Pearl Harbor had been bombed by the Japanese. No one knew what the future would bring. The only news that we received came from the delayed newsreels at the local theater and limited news from the local newspaper, the *Fairbanks Daily News-Miner.*

In June 1942, the Japanese invaded the Aleutian Islands. I couldn't help but remember the comment that was made by that bystander during the Japanese visit in 1937 with the Mitsubishi G3M bomber. Alaska was totally unprepared to defend itself. No one knew how far inland the Japanese would advance. All houses were required to black out all windows and no lights could be seen at night. Blackout wardens patrolled the streets. We anticipated air raids at any time.

There was a tremendous patriotic spirit. Schoolchildren brought their allowances and paper route earnings to school to buy savings bond stamps, 25 cents per stamp, and when a book of stamps was filled, for a total of $17.50, $25.00 could be claimed when the war was over. We drew war bond posters at school and they ended up in the windows of local stores. Collection drives began for aluminum, steel, copper, and rubber tires. Soon military airplanes were coming and going at Ladd Air Force Base on their way to Russia, as part of the Lend-Lease program, to fight on the eastern front against Germany.

I saw the planes coming and going at Ladd Field and I recognized each type from all the pictures and models I collected. I saw Bell P-39s and P-63s, North American B-25s, and Douglas C-47s and A-20s, along with others. I caught glimpses of Russian pilots in downtown Fairbanks. As part of an aviation family, and surrounded by all this activity, all I knew was that I just wanted to be a pilot.

2

Young Pilot

Although I was getting closer to my dream of flying, my teen years were a period in my life when time seemed to stand still. Eventually I was able to work at Wien, cleaning the bellies of airplanes, gassing airplanes, changing oil, and doing whatever nontechnical jobs that needed to be done. In time, one of the mechanics, C. K. Harvey, taught me how to set the valve clearances, like those on a Pratt & Whitney Hornet engine on the Fairchild Pilgrim. By the time I was about fifteen, I was allowed to sit in the airplanes that had newly overhauled engines to run them at different power settings for the eight hour break-in period. It was the closest thing to actually flying at the time and I loved it. I graduated to being able to taxi the airplanes to the gas pit for refueling.

I was soon joined on the flight line by Douglas Millard. Doug started working for Wien Airlines in Nome under the supervision of my uncle Sig and when his mother moved to Fairbanks for a teaching job, he transferred to a flight line job there. We became good friends and as time went on, he was like a brother to Richard and me. We competed for the easy and fun jobs, such as taking garbage to the dump, breaking in overhauled engines, and taxiing airplanes to the gas pit, to avoid the jobs we didn't like, such as cleaning the oil off the bellies of airplanes. Doug eventually went on to a flying career, retiring as a Boeing captain for Wien Air Alaska.

My big opportunity came when Bob Sholton, one of the Wien pilots, took an interest in me. Bob flew the Wien Stinson AT-19 and sometimes he would say to me, "Jump in" when he was on his way to the Yukon River villages. The Stinson was a surplus single engine military version of the civilian Gull Wing Stinson SR Reliants and sometimes it was so full that I just lay on top of the mail sacks. On the return he would let me fly the airplane back to Fairbanks. I was sixteen years old by this time and had already soloed but this was an opportunity to fly the big stuff. The Gull Wing Stinsons were widely used in the Alaska bush at that time because the plane carried a good load and had very strong landing gear. I loved flying the Stinson. Those planes did have one problem, however; the flaps could be positioned only in the full up or full down position. It would have been nice to be able to use partial flaps for takeoff so as to attain additional lift with heavy loads without creating so much drag that climb airspeed could not be reached. I remember seeing pilots try to set the vacuum-actuated flaps to an intermediate position on takeoff by metering the vacuum valve but getting full flap instead. They were able to get off the ground but ended up in the trees off the end of the runway.

A year after my first flights with him, Bob Sholton bought his own AT-19 and let me fly it quite a bit. My dad also bought one, which he later turned over to Wien Airlines. Bob eventually left Wien Airlines and flew DC-3s for Alaska Airlines. In time he and a partner bought two surplus Fairchild C-82s and they started Northern Air Cargo, which grew to be a large cargo carrier throughout Alaska flying DC-6s. I think that my interest in flying was stimulated by my early exposure to all kinds of airplanes and to the pilots, like my father and Bob, who flew them. Just like my father, I loved to fly and so my career choice was clear.

IN 1944, MY PARENTS STARTED ALASKA AIRCRAFT SUPPLY, a parts supply business at Weeks Field in Fairbanks. The business was just beginning to prosper when they had a visit from Joe Crosson. Recently retired from managing Pacific Alaska Airways, a subsidiary of Pan American headquartered in Fairbanks, he was now living in Seattle. Joe had partnered with Charles Babb, whose main business was selling used aircraft at Grand Central Airport in Glendale, California. Their new company was Northwest

Air Service, an aircraft maintenance and parts supply business based at Boeing Field in Seattle. Joe was a very well known early Alaska bush pilot with an impressive record of aviation firsts in Alaska and someone whom my father held in high regard. They were planning to expand to Alaska and Joe proposed a merger with my parents' company. A deal was consummated and our family moved to Seattle.

The plan was for me to travel with Joe back to Seattle but transportation between Alaska and Seattle was somewhat limited in 1945. Joe's good friend Colonel Pat Arnold, Commander of the Tenth Air Rescue, based in Anchorage, offered to pick us up in a North American B-25 and take us as far as Anchorage. Colonel Arnold really stuck his neck out on this one; it was strictly against regulations to transport civilians in military aircraft. Colonel Arnold landed at Weeks Field and offered to show us the inside of the B-25. He "neglected" to deplane us before he started the engines and took off for Elmendorf Air Force Base near Anchorage. Once airborne he said, "Oh, sorry about that. I didn't know you were still onboard." Then Colonel Arnold let me fly most of the way. Little did I know that in a few years I would be going through Air Force pilot training in B-25s. When we arrived in Anchorage and were departing the base, Colonel Arnold had a little trouble explaining to the MPs at the gate how we got on the base to begin with. I don't remember the colonel's explanation but I was impressed and it seemed to satisfy the guard.

In Anchorage, Joe made arrangements with Ray Peterson to catch a ride to Seattle. Ray was the owner of Peterson Airways, later to become Northern Consolidated Airlines after merging with Gillam Airways and Dodson Air Service. Ray had a Lockheed Electra (Amelia Earhart vintage) that he had sold to a customer in Mexico, and Oscar Underhill was ferrying it to Seattle on the way to Mexico. We made the trip in one day with stops at Whitehorse and Prince George. I was able to handle the controls part of the time but when I was riding in the back, I became very airsick and spent most of the time hunched over the portable toilet.

Once in Seattle, I stayed with the Crossons until my family arrived. My folks found a house in the Ballard neighborhood and I attended Ballard High School during my sophomore year. During the school year, I took my first official flying lessons at the old Smith Dairy airport in Kent. Soon after, the flying school moved to Boeing Field where my new instructor was

Sherry Phelps, a cute twenty-something ex-WASP (Women Airforce Service Pilots). I was not into girls yet, especially older women, so I had no trouble concentrating on my flying.

It was a requirement at that time to have a minimum of eight hours from a certified instructor before soloing. So when I had eight hours, ten minutes, I soloed. It was on my sixteenth birthday, a few days before I got my driver's license. I will never forget the thrill of finally being able to fly alone and not have to worry about what the instructor was thinking. Knowing no one could hear me, I sang the Army Air Corps song at the top of my voice, maybe not as loud as I remember hearing Robert Crawford sing it at our house, but loud nonetheless. When I landed, I noticed my mother was a wreck. Apparently, she had nearly fainted when I lifted off on my first take-off. I never understood why she was worried until I watched both my sons solo on their sixteenth birthdays.

My dad left Northwest Air Service that summer and we all returned to Fairbanks. We bought a 1941 DeSoto and drove up the Alcan Highway, now called the Alaska Highway. It wasn't really a highway then since so much of the road was a muddy trail with long stretches of "gumbo" mud, which clung like cement to the underside of the car when it dried. I think it took about two weeks to make the drive since we had to drive east from Seattle to Montana and then head north into Canada via Edmonton and Calgary. Years later, the Hart Highway opened up from Vancouver through the Fraser River Valley to Prince George, cutting off about a thousand miles.

After arriving back in Fairbanks, I was fortunate to be able to work for the airline again. I used the money to build up flying time toward my licenses while I finished high school and I attained my private pilot rating that summer.

Now that the war had ended, Cessna Aircraft was back in the business of building civilian airplanes and the Cessna 140 came on the market. Cessna asked my parents if they would accept the Alaska distributorship for the state. My mother was pressed into service and handled all the sales paperwork. It was a great opportunity for me because I was able to build some time in the brand-new 140s before they were sold. I needed every chance I could get to fly because my time was mostly consumed by working for the airline after school and on weekends. One winter day I thought I would get some flying in during my lunch hour in a demonstrator Cessna on skis that we had. However, before I could fly, the engine needed to be heated with a Herman Nelson heater. I heated the ice off the tail and hurriedly moved the heater to the engine, not realizing that the chimney from the heater was right under the wing. After setting the heater in place and putting the heat tube inside the engine, I looked around to find that the wing was on fire. Fortunately, the metal wing ribs and spar were not damaged but the outer third of the fabric was gone. I was devastated.

ONE DAY IN 1947, DURING MY JUNIOR YEAR, I was sitting in study hall gazing out the window, which I did most of the time. The final approach to Weeks Field passed by the school and suddenly I saw two Stinson L-5s go by. I knew that Sam White and Steve Miskoff were arriving in Fairbanks from the states with these newly acquired World War II–surplus aircraft. When the bell for the lunch hour rang, I tore out of school and ran all the way to the airport. While I was still breathing hard, Sam said to me, "Hey, Merrill, do you want to fly it?" I had received my private license on my seventeenth birthday and had recently checked out in Alaska Flying School's L-5, but I don't think Sam knew that I had flown an L-5 before. I jumped in and made two landings. When I landed, I thanked Sam and ran back to school just in time for the bell. That airplane represented Sam's total worth at the time and he probably borrowed money to buy it. I will never forget his kindness.

Sam was an important person in my life and to this day he is a legend in Alaska. He grew up in Maine and worked on the steam-powered logging tractors that hauled the logs down off the high logging areas. It was a dangerous job but Sam became very good at driving the machines. He was a veteran of World War I, having served on the front lines in the infantry. After the war, he got a job with the Boundary Commission, clearing a border line between Alaska and Canada. Then he went to work for the Alaska Fish and Game Commission. He traveled all over Alaska with dog teams, horses, mules, and on foot, watching for violators of the fish and game laws. He arrested any violators, even friends. This was hard for him to do but for Sam the law was the law. After a few years traveling by dog teams he began to see airplanes fly overhead and the thought entered his mind that maybe there was a better way to get where he was going. He became friends with my father and my uncle Ralph.

Sam bought an airplane with his own money and my dad and Ralph taught him to fly, making him the first flying game warden in Alaska. Using his own airplane drastically cut into his earnings until he was finally able to convince the game commission to finance an airplane. As time went on, Sam was asked not to arrest certain high profile individuals and that did not sit well with him. He eventually left the commission and went to work as a pilot for Wien Airlines. Since Sam knew how to live year-round in the wilds of Alaska he was assigned to take US Geological Survey personnel all over the territory for mapping surveys and would be gone many weeks at a time.

Sam was a skilled and diligent pilot. A brief story, one of so many I know about Sam, illustrates this: Sometime during the early 1940s, I was in the kitchen when the phone rang. My dad answered and it was Leon Vincent at the KAZW aeronautical radio station. He said that Sam White had called in advising of an emergency situation. Sam was flying a Gull Wing Stinson through some turbulence when one of his skis became detached from the forward shock cord and the cable that held the ski in position. The front of the ski went down and the rear of the ski hung up on the bracket on the landing gear where the wheel pant normally is attached, holding the ski in the straight down position. This put the airplane into a spiral that Sam could not control. Then the other ski did the same thing. This allowed him to stop the spiral but he had to use full throttle and hold the control wheel all the way back in his stomach. He was descending but thought he could make it to Circle City. He barely managed to make it and flew at full throttle onto the snow-covered runway. The landing gear broke away and when he came to a stop, he was trapped in the pilot seat. He had onboard 110 gallons of case gas in five-gallon tin cans and some had broken open. Gas was dripping everywhere. He was pulled from the airplane by the local people and fortunately the airplane did not catch fire. Sam was diligent about tying down his loads and this probably saved his life. Sam and my dad constantly stressed the importance of tying down the cargo. Sam was in the hospital for quite a while but eventually made a full recovery.

During the latter part of Sam's flying career, he was based at Hughes on the Koyukuk River. Around 1960, Sam asked me to bring his float-equipped L-5 to Hughes for the summer and then to bring it back to Fairbanks in the fall. I did this several times but once when I was getting the plane ready to depart from Fairbanks, I made a big mistake. My friend Doug

Millard and I were putting the battery in the airplane on the floor under the instrument panel. The fuel line from the overhead fuselage tank passed by just above the battery. I mistakenly hooked up the negative terminal first and then when I attached the positive lead to the battery, the handles of the water pump pliers clipped the fuel line and caused a flaming stream of gas to pour into the fabric-covered belly. I tried to stop the stream of gas but every time I did it I burned my hand. Doug was pouring buckets of water in the belly but the flaming gas continued to float on top of the water. Finally, a Wien mechanic saw our predicament, grabbed a towel from his pickup, dunked it in the water, and told us to wrap it around the gas line. That stopped the source and we were able to put out the fire. Miraculously, the only damage was a small hole in the belly fabric and a ruined cylinder head gauge under the panel. We easily patched the hole and replaced the gauge with one that I happened to have. When I arrived at Hughes and Sam saw the bandages on my hands covering my burns, he said, "You should have let it burn." He was upset about my burns, not about his plane. That captures perfectly who Sam White was. When Sam sold the L-5 years later, the new owner burned up the airplane, like I almost did, the same way.

That fall, when I brought Sam's airplane back to Fairbanks, I had another adventure. As always during the preflight at Hughes, I religiously drained the gas tanks and the fuel strainer to remove the water that often leaked though the gas caps when it rained. I got some water out of both tanks and the strainer and I thought I was all set. On the way to Fairbanks the gas was getting low in the right tank and I thought that it might be a good idea to switch tanks before it was completely empty. Shortly after switching tanks, the engine quit. That was a big surprise. I knew there was still fuel in the first tank but didn't immediately switch back to it. Instead I wasted time trying to get the full tank to feed. Finally, I switched back to the low-fuel tank expecting it to come to life. It did not. I tried everything to get it to start. There was no time to even be scared. My only thought was, *Another fine fix I've got myself into.* I looked for a place to land and the only spot was in the Melozitna River, which was more like a creek than a river. I figured I could touch down in the water and slide up on a gravel bar. As I was setting up for the approach, the engine started to bark but it would run only at idle then would quit when I advanced the throttle. I figured out that I could gradually increase the throttle settings before it would quit and it became apparent that eventually I could get full power back. The question was, would it happen before I ran out of airspace? I had to decide whether to keep messing with the throttle or commit to the river. Having recovered some power caused me to overshoot the river but I got the engine to come back to life just over the trees.

The next year, Sam brought the airplane back from Hughes himself but he did not switch tanks until the tank ran out. By that time he was over the Yukon River and he was able to dead stick it into the river. After that we figured out that even though we were draining all the tanks and the fuel strainer, we were not switching to the other wing tank and draining that line between tank and engine. Another lesson learned.

Sam White was like a second father to me and Richard. In the way he displayed a very high standard of conduct and integrity, he reinforced the guidance we received from our dad and became another important role model for us. When my son Kurt was born, my wife and I asked Sam if he would be Kurt's godfather. He was glad to do it and took his role very seriously.

WE SOLD QUITE A FEW CESSNA 140S BUT when the sales started to decline, my parents turned the distributorship over to Uncle Sig and he formed a new company called Alaska Aeronautical Industries.

In the spring of 1948 my parents decided to move back to Seattle. We drove the same 1941 DeSoto back down the Alaska Highway accompanied by our good friends Doug Millard and his mother, Clara Millard, who were on their way to Iowa. The gumbo mud was as bad as ever and on some stretches we had to be towed through it by D-8 Caterpillars that were stationed along the highway.

The first time we encountered a bad gumbo mud area, the D-8 Caterpillar was idling along the side of the road but the drivers had gone to lunch. Doug, who had just turned sixteen, jumped out of their 1942 Ford and ran over to the tractor. His mother gasped, "Douglas, what do you think you are doing?" He jumped up into the cab and the next thing we saw was a big puff of black smoke blow out of the exhaust. The D-8 spun around and headed for our cars. After we helped him hitch up the cars, he towed them through the mud. When the drivers returned from lunch they were amazed to see a kid doing the driving. We thought that we would be in a lot of trouble but the only thing the driver said was, "Are you making any money?" More cars had gathered behind by then so the drivers took over the duty.

My parents bought a house in the Seattle suburb of Lake Forest Park and I enrolled at the University of Washington to start classes in the fall in aeronautical engineering. I got a job for the summer as gas boy at the nearby Kenmore Air Harbor, a flying service and flight school at the north end of Lake Washington. Most of my pay went to working toward my float rating and commercial license.

My main flight instructor there was Bill Fisk. He was a World War II–B-24 pilot and Kenmore Air's main pilot and instructor for many years. I learned much from Bill. He taught me how to loop and barrel roll the Taylorcraft on floats, along with night takeoffs and landings in that plane. I learned that when the altimeter gets close to what it was reading when the plane was on the water, I should set up a 200- to 300-feet-per-minute rate of descent at an airspeed that sets the touchdown attitude for landing. This is the same procedure that is used for landing on glassy water. That training served me well in later years during my many glassy water landings in Alaska.

When anyone got their float rating it was customary to throw them into the lake. When I got mine, four Kenmore employees dragged me toward the water. I acted limp and lifeless until we got to the T in the dock when I suddenly straightened out, causing the two guys holding my feet to go flying into the lake. I was then able to drag one of the two holding my arms into the lake with me, which was probably not the most sportsman-like thing to do. Tom Wardly and Ted Huntley, two of the guys who went into the water with me, went on to have very distinguished flying careers.

In June 1949 I traveled from Seattle to Wichita, Kansas, with Uncle Sig to pick up two new planes for Wien Airlines. I flew a new Cessna 140A back to Alaska and Uncle Sig flew a Cessna 170. Shortly after arriving in Fairbanks with the new Cessna 140 and returning to my usual summer job at Wien, one of our operations people came to me when I was sweeping floors and said that I had a charter flight. *Whaaaaaaat?* I thought. *I am going to fly a charter?* I had not been hired as a pilot and didn't yet have my commercial license.

I did not know my passenger but we took off and I flew around Fair-banks showing him the sights. When we landed, I found out that he was

Jerry Merrill, the brother of Russell Merrill, my father's good friend who had disappeared in 1929. The airport in Anchorage was named Merrill Field after him. Sometimes I am asked what the relationship is between me and Merrill Field. I would like to say that it was named after me but I don't think that would fly. Every year after our flight, Jerry Merrill sent me a telegram wishing me happy birthday. When he died he willed me $500.

While the rest of the family remained in Seattle, I spent the summer with Sig in Fairbanks working odd jobs for Wien Airlines and getting as much flying time as possible. In July, I passed my commercial check ride with Hawley Evans, founder of Fairbanks Air Service, and a highly respected Alaska pilot.

About the time that I was going to go back home to Seattle to start another year at the University of Washington, I received an offer to fly a North American Navion to Sun Valley, Idaho. Apparently the airplane had been flown up to Alaska by a pilot who thought the route was too sparse and treacherous so he left it with Bob Rice in hopes that he could find someone to fly it back to Sun Valley for him. Bob, who had previously flown for Wien Airlines as chief pilot and had since left to start his own charter service, had two Navions of his own that he was using for charter work so he checked me out in his. My high school friend George Morton flew to Seattle with me and then I delivered the plane to Sun Valley.

That winter, I aborted my college year after completing the first quarter in 1949 to get to work on my instrument rating with Harry Cramer on a Link Trainer he kept in the terminal building at Boeing Field. After I completed my required twenty hours of Link, Harry talked me into working on my Link instructors rating. As part of my training I operated the Link under Harry's supervision, teaching primary instrument students and operating the Link for Boeing pilots and nonscheduled pilots flying to and from Alaska. In March of 1950 I earned my instrument rating, followed a month later by my Link instructors rating. Every time I qualified for a new rating, it was a great feeling, a sense of another stepping stone completed. Then I would focus on the next one.

THE DAY AFTER I PASSED MY INSTRUMENT FLIGHT check, my dad and I flew to Wichita to pick up a brand-new 1949 Cessna 170A that the family had purchased for personal use. While there, we visited the Mooney factory.

The Mooney Mite single seat airplane had recently been introduced and they were very anxious for my dad to fly it. He told them he would take a pass but that his son would like to fly it. They didn't seem to be very enthusiastic about that idea but they reluctantly gave me a cockpit check and turned me loose. I flew it for about thirty minutes and thoroughly enjoyed the experience. Even though it only had 65 hp, it felt like a little fighter. On landing, it didn't touch the ground when I thought it would and as it continued to settle lower, the thought came to me that maybe I forgot to lower the landing gear. When it did touch down it felt like my butt was sliding on the grass. Two days later we flew to Seattle and a few days after that we left for Fairbanks.

Shortly after arriving in Fairbanks with my dad and the new Cessna 170, I returned to my usual summer job at Wien. My mother, brother, and sister drove a new Ford back up the highway as our family returned to Fairbanks to live.

My father, Noel Wien, created history in 1925 by making the first flight north of the Arctic Circle anywhere in the world. He is seen here hand cranking the Standard J-1 at Wiseman, Alaska, for the return trip to Fairbanks.

Famous early Alaska pilot Joe Crosson looking at me in the sled when I was a baby.

This was taken in 1927 in Nome, Alaska, when my dad started Wien Alaska Airways. Note the spare prop tied to the side of the fuselage.

Here I am getting some pretend flying time in the Bull Pup.

In 1938, Howard Hughes stops in Fairbanks flying
a Lockheed Model 14 on a record-breaking
around the world flight of just under four days.
*P341-Cann-7, Alaska State Library, Photographers in Alaska
Photo Collection.*

Photo of the Japanese Mitsubishi G3M visit to Fairbanks in 1937, supposedly on a goodwill tour of Alaska.

Wiley Post lands in Fairbanks in 1933 on his around-the-world record flight of just under eight days.

This is the Avro Avian airplane that ended up in our backyard for us kids to play in, and eventually demolish. It originally belonged to Robert Crawford, composer of the Army Air Corp song who also grew up in Alaska.

Hap Arnold arrived in Alaska with ten Martin B-10s in 1934 to prove the capabilities of the Army Air Service. Arnold later became commanding general of the US Army Air Forces during World War II.

When I was five years old, in 1935, we greeted Wiley Post and Will Rogers arriving on the Chena River near Fairbanks. They were on their way to Point Barrow and points west. They were killed near Point Barrow a few days later. Wiley is getting out of the cockpit and Will Rogers is standing on the right wing. Joe Crosson, famous Alaska aviator, and mechanic, Warren Tillman, are on the dock.

Above: My dad, Noel Wien, and Bob Sholton, 1949, Fairbanks, by the tail of the Wien Fairchild Pilgrim. Bob took me with him on several mail runs in the Stinson AT-19.

Left: Solo day, April 4, 1946, Boeing Field, with my instructor, Sherry Phelps.

One of my first bush flights in the spring of 1950 at the village of Beaver on the Yukon River ice.

The crew I first flew with most frequently the summer of 1950. I'm on the left with Captain Fred Goodwin standing between Wien Airlines' first stewardesses, Betty Windler and Patsy Hornbeck.

I was hired by Pan American in the summer of 1951, and this photo was taken at Juneau, Alaska.

3

Paid to Fly

On June 1, 1950, I was back at my summer job, working on the hangar floor at Wien when our chief pilot, Dick King, said to me, "Do you want to fly the DC-3?" I was flabbergasted. Dick gave me a few landings and signed me off as a qualified DC-3 co-pilot. The biggest airplane that I had flown up to that time was the Stinson AT-19 but the DC-3 felt good to me. The biggest problem I had was getting used to the World War II–technology brakes. I was now a full-fledged airline pilot on the seniority list of Wien Alaska Airlines.

The first captain I flew with was Fred Goodwin. I have been so fortunate to be able to fly with captains who made the effort to share their knowledge and experience. So many early captains in the industry told their co-pilot to just sit there and not to touch anything. Cockpit resource management (CRM) was not yet in vogue. But Fred was different. He gave me responsibility and didn't over-instruct, letting me figure things out on my own as much as possible.

Fred kept me in the left seat most of the time but he did not make it easy for me. The first thing he did was to tell me I had to get a crew cut. Then he said that whenever I saw him patting his shirt pocket, I was to whip out the cigarettes that I was carrying for him and light one with the lighter that

I also was required to carry. It was a small price to pay for such a great education. When I screwed up he made sure that I did not forget it. He was very accomplished in the scolding area but that resulted in cementing his teachings in my mind. He also had some fun with me. When Fred made a less than stellar landing, he would put his captain hat on me and say, "Go greet the passengers as they get off the airplane." I flew with other captains that first summer but there is no doubt that of all of them, Fred taught me the most.

When I became a captain I always tried to be the same kind of captain that Fred was for me. I made a big effort to pass on my knowledge if a newer pilot showed the eagerness to learn and, like Fred, I let them fly most of the time. I made comments and subtle suggestions and when I noticed improvements, I complimented them. This seemed to stimulate more eagerness to learn and I loved seeing the results. From Fred's example, I learned that the really good instructors know when to talk and when to let the students learn by making mistakes. If an instructor is talking all the time, it becomes a distraction and the student is not able to concentrate on flying. I also felt, as did Fred, that if a student made a serious mistake, it should be emphasized in no uncertain terms.

In the early days, the captain was the captain and there was no question about who was in command because he carried the final responsibility for the safety of the aircraft. In the summer of 1950 the airline decided to hire for the first time two trained flight attendants (we called them stewardesses back then) from a training academy in the states. They were well trained but one of them could get a little testy. During one flight with mostly tourists onboard, she decided that she did not want to go any higher because her tourists could not see the wildlife. She came to the cockpit and rolled the trim tab forward. I thought, *Oh dear, she knows not what she has done. Fred Goodwin is the captain and he is not going to be willing to give up command of the ship.* Fred jumped out of his seat and threw her out of the cockpit, locking the cockpit door behind her. She hollered and banged on the locked door in front of all the passengers.

I think that was her first awareness of how the chain of command worked. Apparently the training school did not cover that subject.

I like to think back to how things were when I first started flying. You did not see any NO ADMITTANCE signs anywhere in the airport. The cockpit doors were not locked, and we used to allow the tourists to come to the cockpit and sit in the co-pilot's seat to get a good look at bear, caribou, mountain sheep, and wolves while flying through the John River Pass in the Brooks Range on the way to Point Barrow.

That summer was one of the worst I have seen for forest fires. We would sometime fly an entire trip on instruments due to heavy smoke. One day I was flying with our chief pilot, Dick King, and I was in the left seat as we were arriving back in Fairbanks. The approach was from the radio range station east of Ladd Field. It was necessary to proceed from the range station on a certain heading over Ladd Field until a certain amount of time was up. If we did not see the lights of the Squadron Club on Cushman Street, we made a missed approach. I saw the lights and then the runway and proceeded to set my final approach. All of a sudden I realized that we were too high and I used up a lot of runway at Weeks Field. I was embarrassed, but the next day the same thing happened to Dick as he landed in Fairbanks. I then discovered how smoke can cause a kind of refracted sight picture. Another lesson learned.

As a new pilot at Wien Airlines, I also started flying the bush in the Cessna 170, Cessna 195, and the Noorduyn Norseman. I loved to fly any kind of airplane and wanted to gain as much experience as possible. Like any young person, I'm sure I thought I was a better pilot than I was. On one of my first trips, my dad came to the airplane to check that I had properly tied down the load and that I had the proper emergency equipment onboard. Just before he shut the door he said, "Remember, always bring the airplane back." I don't think he meant on a truck either. Those words came to mind whenever I started to push the weather or wondered if landing conditions were good enough. I probably took some chances that I shouldn't have and had some close calls but I was lucky and in time I became more cautious.

It has been written that Noel Wien was sometimes called a fair-weather pilot. He did occasionally take calculated risks but his philosophy was that it was much easier to explain why he did not get his passengers to their destination on time than to try to explain to friends and relatives why the passengers were killed or injured. He was among the few early pioneers who survived while accomplishing many historic firsts.

THE AIRLINE HAD RECENTLY ACQUIRED HARRY CRAMER'S LINK Trainer and it was in a Quonset hut by the hangar. Before Wien Airlines had arranged for a place to set it up, the trainer was stored in the basement of our house. This was an opportunity for me to put in many hours flying simulated instruments and I made the most of it.

Because I had my Link instructors rating, I became the approved operator for the required Link time for our pilots. Harry Cramer had taught me the new way to use the automatic direction finder (ADF) azimuth for approaches. The old way was to keep the rotatable azimuth on zero and mentally calculate the bearing to and from the station by adding the heading to the relative bearing and then subtracting 180 degrees if it was over 360 degrees. The new way was to rotate the azimuth to the compass heading, which meant that the needle then pointed to the bearing to the station, and the tail of the needle was on the bearing from the station. All you had to do was look at the needle instead of doing all the mental arithmetic. It was much simpler but the captains I worked with resisted learning this new procedure. They were very experienced, very competent pilots but as the saying goes, it's hard to teach an old dog new tricks. Every time I reached for the rotatable knob during flights, the captains would slap my hand.

The original ADF instrument had a rotatable knob because the route structure on the maps originally showed the courses in true north. In order to convert that to compass headings, you had to move the knob to the magnetic variation that showed on the maps for your location. In fact, the knob had VAR (variation) marked on it. After the mapped routes were changed to the magnetic courses, the rotating azimuth was slaved to the heading indicator so you did not have to keep rotating it. I still have one of the old ADF instruments and it is a treasure to me.

Even with my skills in the Link, the captains made sure I knew that just because I was a hotshot in that area, I still had a lot to learn. But I already knew this and it became even more clear to me as winter came and I continued to fly part-time in much more difficult conditions. On one trip, the captain put me in the left seat for the entire flight. The weather was terrible at Kotzebue and the night approach required a circle to the landing runway because of the wind direction. We had a big load of ice on the windshield so we had to open the sliding part of the windshield (called the clear view window) to see. The air noise in the cockpit made it hard for me to hear the captain's airspeed call-outs. I started my left turn from downwind and because I lost sight of the runway, I just had to hope that my lineup with it would be close. When the runway reappeared, the lineup was good. Just before crossing the approach end, I barely heard the captain call 85, which was too slow with the load of ice we had on the airplane. I had forgotten to carry extra airspeed for the ice so when I eased the power off to flare, the airplane stalled a few feet above the ground. I just sucked the wheel all the way back and, surprisingly, the airplane made a nice three-point touchdown. But because we had a strong quartering crosswind and the braking action was poor, I had to keep jabbing the left throttle to keep it straight. My foot was shaking badly when I tried to apply the brake for directional control and we just barely got stopped before the runway ended. I could not figure out why my captain did not give me some advice or lend me a hand. I had clearly been way over my head in those conditions and had no idea why he let me make the approach in the first place. It was not normal for a captain to put a newer pilot in a situation like that and I can't explain what he was thinking.

IN THE SPRING OF 1951, MY PARENTS' GOOD friend and former Wien Airlines pilot Herm Joslyn came to visit during one of his trips to Fairbanks. He was now a Pan American captain based in Seattle. During the visit, he said Pan American was having trouble finding pilots and asked me if I would be interested in flying for them. I was dumbfounded at the thought of possibly being a Pan Am pilot flying the DC-4. I expressed interest and a short time later I had an interview and received a job offer from Ralph Savory, the chief pilot of the Seattle division. My only concern was that I had two weeks left in my sophomore year and would lose my draft deferment if I quit school. Ralph emphasized that they would be hiring more pilots in that time and that seniority would be very important. He assured me that he could get a deferment for me because Pan American was crucial to the support of the Korean War. It was a tough decision to quit school early but I did, and left for Seattle. It turned out to be the wrong decision but sometimes fate calls the shots for a reason.

After two weeks of ground school in Seattle and two days flight training, I was checked out as co-pilot in the DC-4. I turned twenty-one a few days before I started flying and thought I was the youngest pilot Pan American had ever hired. I later found out that Jack Burke, who was one of my instructors, was actually the youngest, having been hired at age eighteen. The Pan Am stewardesses seemed to be intrigued by the "boy aviator" and I got a lot of attention from them, though I will admit I was very bashful amongst so many beautiful girls.

I flew two trips to Honolulu and two trips to Alaska a month and I was making three hundred dollars a month—one hundred dollars less than I was making at Wien but I supposed that flying a DC-4 to Hawaii was worth it. I flew with some excellent captains at Pan Am, particularly Jack Burke, Jimmy Stewart, Dick Ogg, Dick Hawley, Roy Holm, Frank Fuller, and, of course, Herm Joslyn. Herm was a wonderful mentor to me. Very often when I flew with him, he would give me his leg in addition to mine. He was also captain on my first flight to Honolulu. There were four legs on the Seattle-Portland-Honolulu route and four pilots so we each got a leg in the left seat.

When I first walked up the stairs into the Moana Hotel in Honolulu, I could not believe my eyes. Looking through the lobby, I saw that it had no wall on the ocean side and to me, a young man from Alaska, the palm trees and the beautiful surf made it look like a fantasy land. I could not wait to get to the beach. Not too long after getting settled on a beach towel in the sand, I heard Herm say, "Well, Merrill, I think you have had enough sun for the day." After arguing about it for a while, I reluctantly went back to the hotel. In a few hours I developed the most painful sunburn that I had ever experienced. Even on the ground I had lessons to learn as a new pilot.

On one of my flights with Herm Joslyn, it was my shift in the left seat, maintaining the heading directed by the navigator as we flew from Honolulu to Portland. As usual two crew were on duty for two hours while the other two slept. During my shift, Captain Joslyn was asleep on his cot. It was a beautiful night with a full moon and the stars were shining brightly. Scattered clouds below reflected the silvery moonlight. I could not believe that I was so fortunate to be where I was. I suddenly realized I had been staring out the window and shook myself from my daydream. Checking the instrument panel, I noticed that the number four auxiliary tank had quite a bit more fuel in it than the other seven tanks. I thought that it would be nice to make the tanks more even so I put all four engines on the one auxiliary tank to get it down to an equal level. It was such a beautiful night and I soon returned to daydreaming. Then, guess what? All four engines quit. The number four auxiliary tank had emptied in no time. I hurriedly pulled the throttles back, put all four engines back on the main tanks, and turned on the respective boost pumps. The engines gradually came back to life as I eased the throttles back to cruise power. About that time, I turned around to see Captain Joslyn standing in the aisle looking through the curtain. He looked around long enough to see that everything had returned to normal and then crawled back into his cot. He did not say a word. Kinda wish he had.

GROWING UP IN FAIRBANKS, FRESH FRUIT AND VEGETABLES had to be canned for winter consumption. My grandparents had a huge garden and greenhouse and canning took place in earnest every fall. We had a limited supply of fresh milk, which we mixed with powdered milk from the dairies. Often we simply drank powdered milk. After being in Seattle I could not get enough of fresh milk, fruit, and vegetables. Whenever I was able to bring fresh food and milk home from Seattle, it was a big hit.

The first time I brought a suitcase full of milk cartons home, I did not pay attention to how I packed them. Shortly after takeoff, the stewardess came up to the cockpit to say that there was a lot of white liquid draining down the aisle from where the crew bags were. I thought, *Oh, no.* I went back to the crew baggage storage and saw that the milk was flowing out of my suitcase. As we climbed, the reduced pressure in the cabin had caused the milk to flow from the top of the cardboard containers and the other crew bags piled on top did not help. That was very embarrassing and it took me a while to mop it up. Another lesson learned.

AFTER I HAD BEEN WITH PAN AM FOR a while, I had a few days off so I went to Fairbanks and rode around with Fred Goodwin on a tourist flight to Nome and Kotzebue. When we departed Kotzebue for the flight back to Fairbanks, Fred said, "Take the left seat." It had been about four months since I had flown the DC-3 but I knew Fred would keep me out of trouble. As I got in the left seat he put the jump seat down and sat in it. I could not believe my eyes. I don't know if he was confident in me or confident that Gerry Bolms, the co-pilot, would be able to correct any deviations. The DC-3 felt good but like a much smaller airplane after flying the DC-4. At this time in my life, I was in hog heaven at Pan Am but circumstances can change very fast, as I was soon to discover.

4

In the Army Now

In September 1951, I got a call from my parents telling me that a draft notice had arrived in the mail. Right away, I went to Ralph Savoy with the news and he said that he would take care of it. He petitioned General Hershey, the head of the Selective Service, but my request for deferment was refused. I then had a choice: I could be drafted into the Army and serve for two years or I could choose to enlist in the Air Force and serve five years. I could not imagine doing anything but flying in the military so I chose the Air Force. I still wonder whether I made a mistake because many of my friends decided to take the draft and they ended up serving in Alaska at Fairbanks, home every night and out in two years.

I received a military leave of absence from Pan American. When I went to work for Pan Am, I had taken a six-month leave of absence from Wien Airlines with the thought that I would get some good experience for a short time and would probably come back to Wien a better pilot. Because I was drafted short of my six months with Pan Am, I received a military leave of absence from Wien Airlines as well as Pan Am. It was comforting to know that when I was released from the Air Force, I could take my pick of which airline to return to and keep my original hiring date.

I enlisted in the Air Force at Ladd Field along with Dave Vincent, a friend from Fairbanks. I immediately applied for pilot training in the cadet program but found out that because I had not completed my sophomore year of college, I did not meet the requirements. I actually did have two years of college because of the extra quarter I had at the University of Washington, but because I did not get any credit for the semester I almost completed at the University of Alaska, I came up short. I was devastated. I felt that I should have stayed at the University of Alaska for the two weeks left to complete the semester, even if it cost me some seniority with Pan Am.

That began my ongoing attempt to somehow qualify for cadet training. With my parents' help, we requested assistance from Bob Bartlett, our representative in Congress from the Territory of Alaska. He contacted General Twining, the commander of the Alaskan Air Command, to see if he could help. We also submitted many letters of recommendation, along with my flying experience and ratings. We were hoping that my flying background would qualify for the missing two weeks of college. I actually had more than two years of college but because I quit before the end of the semester, none of that semester counted. General Twining agreed and set things in motion for the Air Force to accept my qualifications for the program.

Normally new enlistees would come to Ladd Field right out of Air Force basic training in Biloxi, Mississippi. The personnel at Ladd Field decided that rather than sending me and Dave to Mississippi, they would send us to infantry basic training at Fort Richardson, near Anchorage. The next class was to begin in two weeks so Dave and I were put to work at Ladd Field, doing KP, peeling potatoes, cleaning toilets, and painting rooms. I remember looking out the latrine window and seeing a Pan American DC-4 landing. It had been only about three weeks since I had been flying DC-4s. I wondered, *Where did I go wrong to end up here in this latrine?*

When the next infantry basic training class started, Dave and I found ourselves at Fort Richardson. I was determined to do the best that I possibly could. I ended up having the highest rifle score that the training detachment had ever had. I guess I had an advantage because in college I had joined the rifle club at the University of Alaska where I learned how to shoot. I was soldier of the week three out of four times that grading took place.

As glad as I was to be in Alaska, I sometimes wished that they had sent me to Biloxi because I was cold all the time. When I was lying on the freezing ground learning how to shoot an M1 rifle, my thoughts often drifted off to lying on the beach near the Moana Hotel in Honolulu. You might call it shock cooling.

After completing infantry basic training Dave and I were sent back to Ladd Field. When we got there, it became apparent that we didn't have any clear assignment there—I don't know why—so they said we could go off base after checking in every morning. If they could not find anything for us to do, we were released but we remained on standby and were supposed to stay fairly close to the base. One morning I left the base and reported for duty at Wien Airlines. They sent me on a flight to Fort Yukon and as I was landing there, Dave Vincent called on our HF frequency, 5652.5 KC from his dad's aeronautical radio station. He said that the base had called and that we were to report immediately. *Oh boy*, I thought. *I'm in big trouble.* When I returned to Ladd Field, I was restricted to the base for two weeks. All I did during that time was lie on a cot all day long, getting up only to go to meals. All I could think about was how short of pilots Pan Am and Wien Airlines were. Eventually I was assigned to the mail room sorting mail into mailboxes, which only resulted in a lot of sinus problems from mail dust.

I almost got in trouble again a couple of months later when I was at the airport and one of the Wien pilots, Dave Bronaugh, asked me if I would like to take his flight to Eagle in a Cessna 195, which would require me to remain in Eagle overnight due to darkness. He did not want to be gone overnight but I was always eager to fly so I took a chance on being AWOL again. The only hitch was that I was scheduled for guard duty at eight o'clock the next morning.

Figuring I could get back in time, I took the trip. When I arrived at Eagle, I drained the oil and put the wing and engine covers on for the night, which was standard procedure for cold weather. I placed the oil can by the stove in the log cabin where I stayed because it was important to have warm oil the next morning.

It was still dark when I got up at 4:00 A.M. and I headed for the airport with the warm can of oil. I lit a fire pot and placed it inside the motor cover with the oil can alongside. I stood by the plane, patiently waiting for the engine to be warm enough to start and to make sure the wind did not blow the engine cover into the flame. I knew about several airplanes that had burned because the pilot went to the roadhouse for a cup of coffee while waiting for the engine to get warm. It ended up taking me much longer to

TRAINING DETACHMENT
FORT RICHARDSON, ALASKA
APO 949, c/o Postmaster
Seattle, Washington

27 November 1951

SUBJECT: Outstanding Trainee

TO: Commanding Officer
        Fort Richardson
        Fort Richardson, Alaska

1. Reference is made to our conversation of 17 November 195?
relative to the outstanding performance of Private Noel M. Wien,
10730300, Headquarters, 5001 Composite Wing, Ladd Air Force Base,
Alaska, on TDY with this organization for completion of basic tra
ing.

2. During the conduct of the past seven (7) weeks Private
has displayed an outstanding ability to perform his duty assignme
Initially Wien was appointed hut leader by his platoon sergeant.
servation of this assignment revealed dependability and an abilit
to have his men willingly work with and for him. His attitude to
ward the training and the military way has always been excellent.
In addition, he achieved the highest score to date on the rifle
range as compared to men previously trained in this unit. Privat
Wien was chosen as soldier of the week three (3) out of four (4)
times the selection was made. A desire has been expressed by Wien
to further his career by attending the Air Cadet School.

                        WILBUR F PRICE
                        1st Lt   Inf
                        Commanding

From First Lieutenant Wilbur F. Price, the commander of the training detachment at Fort Richardson near Anchorage, Alaska. I had tried to excel in Army basic training and apparently my efforts caught Price's attention. When he asked me what my goals were, I explained that I was trying to gain admission into Air Force pilot training, and he wrote this letter of recommendation for me.

heat the engine than I had anticipated and I barely made it back to the base in time for guard duty.

The one bright spot in my time at Ladd was the Link Trainer operation on the base. When I found out about it, I paid a visit to the sergeant in charge. He was delighted to hear that I had a Link instructors rating and arranged for me to transfer to his department. At last I was doing something that I was trained for. The rated pilots on the base were required to fly the Link a certain amount of time each month if they wanted to get flight pay. I was a little nervous when I had my first bird colonel in the trainer, intimidated by the many ribbons on his uniform but I worked hard to do my job well.

I was surprised how incompetent some of these pilots were but I guess their desk jobs interfered with flying activities. It seemed to me that the Air Force did not have career professional pilots. About the time that they became very qualified pilots, they were either released from the service because their time was up or, if they wanted to be career officers, they were required to put flying aside and take on management duties. I believe the accident rate per flight hour of Air Force pilots was probably much higher than that of commercial airline pilots. I think that eventually the Air Force began to realize the importance of keeping pilots in a high state of currency and they let experienced pilots fly the airplanes and management-trained officers run the Air Force, especially in the Strategic Air Command and the fighter squadrons.

I HAD BEEN IN THE AIR FORCE FOR about a year when the requirements for cadets were reduced to a high school education. I was soon accepted into the cadet program and received orders to report to Marana Air Base, near Tucson, Arizona, in August 1952. The Air Force primary pilot training bases were actually civilian contract bases manned with civilian instructors and personnel; however, there were Air Force pilots on duty to administer check rides during the courses. A friend and I drove my 1948 Plymouth from Seattle to Marana. We arrived at the base about the time that the morning period airplanes were all returning. The traffic pattern had three arrival levels to fly and the sky was filled with noisy T-6s. It was very impressive and I will never forget that sight and sound.

The T-6 was called an AT-6 during World War II because it was used as an advanced trainer at that time. Primary flight training had utilized smaller, less complicated trainers, such as the Boeing Stearman, Fairchild PT-19, or the Ryan PT-22. Then basic training was usually in the Vultee BT-13, followed by advanced training in the AT-6. During the Korean War, the Training Command decided to just start with the advanced trainer for primary training. I was impressed that pilot applicants were able to solo the T-6 after as few as twenty hours, even if they had never flown in an airplane before. I had a big advantage.

During the initial paperwork process, a question on a form asked if I had any previous flight time. I put down yes and described, as requested, the type of experience and hours that I had accrued. That was a mistake. Word got around and the upper class cadets had a field day with me. Often, as we marched to the cafeteria, the upperclassmen would wait for me. Pulling me aside, they would proceed with the hazing. "So, Wien, you think you know how to fly, do you? Well, let's see if you know how to fly a traffic pattern." They directed me to make engine noises and run a flight pattern with arms extended while yelling out the appropriate checklists.

I seemed to be the one that flew the most traffic patterns but all the lower-class cadets would be asked questions from time to time and we had to memorize the required answers. If we were asked, "What time is it?" we replied:

"Sir, I am greatly embarrassed and deeply humiliated that due to circumstances over which I have no control, the inner workings and hidden mechanisms of my chronometer are in such inaccord with the great sidereal movement by which time is commonly reckoned that I cannot with any degree of accuracy state the exact time. However, without fear of being too far wrong, I will say that it is x minutes and x seconds and x ticks past the hour." Another question might be: "What is the definition of a duck?" "Sir, one of its legs is both the same."

Or, "What is the definition of leather?" "If the fresh skin of an animal, clean and divested of all hair, fat, and other extraneous matter be submerged in a dilute solution of tannic acid, a chemical combination ensues. The gelatinous tissue of the skin is converted into a non-putrescible substance impervious to and insoluble in water. This, sir, is leather."

When eating a meal, if we needed to get a drink of water we marched to the water container and said, "Sir, aviation cadet Wien, Noel Merrill, reports to Colonel Temprite for a drink of water, sir."

When unable to answer a question asked by an upperclassman, the response would be, "Sir, not being informed to the highest degree of accuracy I hesitate to articulate for fear I might deviate from the true course of rectitude; in short, sir, I am a very dumb fourth classman, sir, and I do not know, sir."

My eighth grade teacher had required that all her students learn a different poem every week and recite it to the class. I think that experience was a big help in memorizing these useless phrases.

SINCE I HAD PREVIOUS EXPERIENCE, THEY ASSIGNED OUR assistant operations officer to take me on and prepare me for a military check ride, which was required to solo in less than twenty hours. They wanted as many pilots as possible to qualify to solo so they could put more planes in the air and get more utilization sooner.

When flying began, my total flight time was already about 1,500 hours. A couple of the instructors in our class had less time than that. I was assigned to a great instructor, Chuck Wilson. He taught me acrobatics that were not in the curriculum, such as how to do a loop on top of an Immelmann or how to do three slow rolls in succession without the engine quitting. Chuck was a great pilot and taught me a lot about precision and accuracy.

My operations officer for this training was George Truman. I recognized his name from hearing about an around-the-world flight that he and Clifford Evans had made in two Piper Super Cruisers a few years earlier. Truman was qualified in the T-6 but not very well versed in the curriculum since he was not one of the regular instructors. I remember he tried to show me a snap roll and I happened to be looking at the airspeed indicator when he yanked the stick back. At 160 mph the G force was quite high before it finally snapped. Fortunately the wings stayed on.

After eleven hours of training in the T-6, I was put up for solo. Normally, solos happened at between twenty and thirty hours and any solo at less than twenty hours of dual instruction required a military check ride before a pilot would be authorized to solo. My military check pilot's name was Captain Charles Wareham. He was all business and made no attempt to put me at ease, even though I was quite nervous. My first mistake came when he asked me to do a one-turn spin and I did a two-turn spin, which was hard to do because the recovery procedure used up one turn. As soon as I did it, I could feel the fire coming out of Captain Wareham's mouth on the back of my head. He sure knew how to make you feel like the stupidest pilot in the world. After that, I was quite shaken and found it hard to do anything right. I was sure that I had flunked the ride. When we landed, I reported to his desk with a salute and he said, "Nice ride, Wien," and he shook my hand with a big smile. What a surprise and a great relief. I guess he wanted to know how I performed under pressure. Not very good I would say but he seemed satisfied. I soloed the next day at the Red Rock auxiliary field and, according to tradition, was later thrown into the swimming pool.

Soon it was time for dinner and another tradition. As we sat down, an upperclassman yelled out, "Have any of you dodos soloed today?"

I was feeling very relieved and happy that I had been able to solo and almost forgot that I was supposed to stand on a chair and yell out to all in the cafeteria, "At ease, at ease, at ease! To all you dodos who are hampered by sluggish reflexes and have not been accorded the privilege of making like a bird alone, I soloed today at 1,400 hours! My instructor insists that I am the hottest rock at Marana Air Base! I am no longer a slipshod neophyte but a full-fledged birdman of the United States Air Force!"

I probably flubbed my lines somewhat with all the hooting and jabs from upperclassmen, but I got through it. I think that I was as thrilled as I had been when I first soloed the Luscombe at Boeing Field six years earlier. It might seem an anticlimactic experience to solo after 1,500 hours of experience but I have to say that I felt it was quite an accomplishment.

The training that I received at Marana Air Base was some of the best training that I ever had and required a high degree of precision. I think that the checklist for the T-6 was more comprehensive than for the Pan Am DC-4. Flawless precision with bank angles and airspeed was required, especially when arriving back at the base and transitioning through the three levels of the pattern.

Before beginning the instrument flight portion of the program we were required to take Link training. After my initial experience with divulging my flying experience, I hesitated to talk about my Link skills. My instructor turned out to be a nice woman. After the initial briefing, she put me in the Link, turned it on, and unlatched the supporting straps. She got on the mike and started telling me what she wanted me to do. "Make a standard rate 360-degree turn to the right and roll out on the entry heading." I did that as precisely as I could. "Make a turn to the left." I did. "OK, now start a climb of 500 feet per minute. While climbing, start a right turn, level off, and then descend 500 feet per minute. Stop turn and level off." I was able to make the needles go exactly where she wanted them. Then there was a long silence. Eventually she opened the hood, put the trainer back in the straps, and shut the Link down. She asked me to get out of the trainer.

She said, "OK, what's the deal?"

I said, "I don't understand."

"Are you here to test me?" she asked.

"Oh, I guess I need to tell you that I used to be a Link instructor. As a matter of fact, I used to be an airline pilot."

That was the last time that I had to get into the Link. When I showed up for additional training we just chatted about flying. She wanted to know all about Alaska.

When it came time to fly under the hood in the T-6, I had a very unpleasant experience. My instructor was in the front seat and I was sitting in the backseat with the hood down. After we lined up on the runway, I was required to keep the needle in the center and keep the directional gyro on the exact runway heading to make an instrument takeoff.

Little did I know that while my instructor was doing the run-up he had noticed a friend of his, who was also with an instrument student. They had signaled that they would meet over the hill for some fun. I did the instrument takeoff and was climbing out when my instructor said, "I got it." The airplane proceeded to go through some violent maneuvers. I unlatched the instrument hood to find that we were in a dogfight. We were on his tail and then he was on our tail. I knew that in the primary program, no airplanes were allowed to be anywhere near one another but I sure enjoyed the dogfight. About that time, another T-6 came out of the sky and it turned out to be an instrument check ride with an Air Force check pilot. He got both our aircraft numbers.

That began a very emotional experience for me. I knew that both the instructors were in big trouble. They got together and mapped out a plan for an excuse of their behavior. I can't remember the details of the story they concocted, but I do remember that it was far-fetched. They asked me and the other student to tell the same story. I reluctantly went along with it but when I was interviewed and they asked me to swear on the Bible about the authenticity of my story, I couldn't do it. The cover story was blown and the instructors were severely penalized. I had a very high regard for my instructor's flying ability and I hated to betray him, but I thought my self-respect took precedence.

Sometime later, the four of us in his charge were set up to do a triangular cross country. My instructor was assigned for air watch duty at Deming, New Mexico, to check us arriving there before proceeding to Safford Regional Airport and then back to Marana to complete the triangle. At the briefing he said, "I've got an idea." All I could think was, *Oh, no. Now what?* He said that if I would "get disoriented" and keep flying toward El Paso, he would "attempt" to catch me and we just might end up with a great overnight in El Paso. I wasn't sure that I wanted to get a poor grade for this cross country if they thought I got lost and missed the Deming checkpoint. However, if they were able to determine that it was a setup, the repercussions might have been even worse.

My instructor wasn't the only one who sometimes liked to break the rules. During our flight, my friend Willard Teel and I had a lot of fun dogfighting and flying formation, which we absolutely were not supposed to be doing. To cover our tracks, we both made up fake flight reports during the flight showing en route times and checkpoint times that verified that we were never near one another. I don't think we realized how serious all this could be. Following regulations is a very important part of military training and it could have meant washing out of pilot training, or having to walk tours for the duration of our training with no time off base.

When we got over Deming, I chickened out. I did not have the courage to activate my instructor's plan. So much for a great time in El Paso.

There were other cadets who also enjoyed a little unauthorized fun. One afternoon, two cadets, one of whom had about seventy-five hours civilian time, decided to meet quite a ways from the practice area for some dogfighting and formation. The one with previous flying time demonstrated to his friend how to do a low level slow roll. Not to be outdone, his friend also did one but didn't know how much altitude could be lost if the slow roll was not done properly. On the recovery, he lost so much altitude that he hit a cactus and knocked about five feet off the right wing. The impact knocked the stick out of his hand and he knew he was going to crash. He put his arms in front of his head and waited for the inevitable. Seconds went by and no crash, so he looked up to see that he was flying level. There was about a foot remaining of the right aileron, which had jammed down on impact, giving enough left stick to keep the airplane level. He grabbed the stick and started thinking of an excuse. The other pilot distanced himself from the area as fast as he could. I was on the parade field when we saw the T-6 fly over with five feet gone from the right wing. We could not believe that it was still flying. The pilot wanted to land on the wheels but the powers that be would not let him. So, with the help of a chase plane, he was able to belly the airplane at a higher approach speed than normal. He tried to explain to his commanders that he had had a midair collision but he could not explain the cactus lodged in the wing. Eventually, the whole story came out and both pilots were punished. They were not washed out of the program, but they both had to walk tours on the parade ground during their off time and on weekends for the rest of the program and it continued after moving to advanced training.

As graduation neared, we were asked if we wanted to move on to jets or to multiengines. I requested multiengine school because I planned to return to airline flying after discharge. My good friend from primary flight training, Stanley McCaig, and I were sent to Reese Air Force Base in Lubbock, Texas.

MY FIRST FORTY HOURS OF TRAINING AT REESE were done in the North American T-28A. We were the first class to fly the T-28. I guess this was to get us used to the tricycle gear before flying the bomber and probably to save on some training costs.

After a few hours of formation training in the T-28, I was sent up solo with two other airplanes flown with instructors. Normally this involved just dual formation—join-ups and peel offs in V and echelon formations but I think the instructors decided to see if I could do more. We flew some turns in a V formation and then an echelon formation, which were both pretty straightforward. Then some unscheduled training started. I was number three as they peeled off for some in-trail acrobatics. I hung on for dear life. Then they put me in the lead and told me they would follow me in trail. Since these instructors seemed to be game for anything, I took a chance and when I peeled off I rolled completely around and up again and positioned myself in the number three position. I could see that they were looking all over for me and finally discovered that I was on their right wing. They never said a word to me about the flight after we landed and there was no customary debriefing.

After forty hours in the T-28, we started training in the B-25, the plane that is most remembered for the Doolittle raids on Japan flying off the USS *Hornet* in April 1942. I remembered handling the controls in Colonel Arnold's B-25 in 1945 and was sure looking forward to flying that famous airplane as a pilot.

The training with Air Force instructors was much more relaxed than primary and it was great fun. We flew a lot of formation and several long cross-country flights. Because of my DC-3 and DC-4 civilian time, I found the B-25 easy to fly. The B-25 was a twin engine bomber and much of the training was learning how to handle the airplane on one engine. It was a nice flying airplane but the hardest part was getting used to the sensitivity of the brakes.

Toward the end of my B-25 training, I was notified that I was being shipped to Korea to fly the Douglas B-26. In Korea, the B-26 (known as the A-26 during World War II) was used for bombing and strafing—a very dangerous assignment. But, luckily for me, the Korean War ended about a month before graduation and I received new orders to fly the Fairchild C-119F Boxcar at Charleston Air Force Base in South Carolina.

As disappointed as I had been to not be able to get into flight training immediately after enlisting, I now began to think that maybe the Lord was looking after me. If I had gotten into flight training a year earlier, I probably would have flown a lot of combat in Korea and maybe not survived.

5

Aircraft Commander

After receiving my wings and a second lieutenant commission, I had thirty days off between assignments so I went home to Fairbanks. While I was there, I flew about ten trips for the airline. It was nice to get a little extra money after the $97 a month I had been paid as a cadet.

My mother came to Lubbock with me and we drove the Plymouth to Charleston. I was assigned to the 456th Troop Carrier Wing, 746th Troop Carrier Squadron. My classmate, Stanley McCaig, and I checked in with operations. The assistant operations officer, Captain Harold Mitchell, gave us a nice reception and briefed us on what to expect. Stan and I then proceeded to find a room at the Bachelor Officers Quarters (BOQ) and we became roommates. We were soon scheduled for ground school in the C-119 and after some local flight training, we qualified as co-pilots in the C-119.

The wing was assigned many trips to Pope Air Force Base at Fort Bragg, North Carolina, to drop paratrooper trainees from the 82nd Airborne on the drop zones nearby. I flew my first trip to Pope with Captain Harold Mitchell. That was my first experience flying formation with large aircraft. When we peeled off for a 360-degree overhead approach to landing, I was shocked at how close we were to the airplane ahead of us. I once had had a bad experience in Fairbanks landing a Cessna 140 too closely behind a C-46. My plane had flipped upside down on final and I barely recovered in time for landing. I sure would like to see more primary training in how to recover from unintentional inverted flight. I have seen too many pilots try to recover by pulling back on the stick instead of pushing forward and rolling the airplane upright. I soon found out that if the airplane ahead of you was the same size or smaller the roll tendency was controllable. It was also important not to be lower on the glide path than the airplane ahead since the disturbed air from all the airplanes was deflected down. The size difference between the airplanes was the most important consideration, though.

I think I was at Charleston about three months when a request came down from wing headquarters asking for a volunteer to go to Ladd Field, Fairbanks Alaska, to attend Arctic survival training. Well, guess who volunteered?

They gave me airline tickets to go to Fairbanks with an overnight in Seattle, where I looked up my friend Dick Aimes, who had been my roommate when I flew for Pan Am. That evening, we were driving in his car when we heard on the radio that there had been an accident at Pope involving a C-119. The radio announcer read the names of the crew. The co-pilot was my roommate, Stanley McCaig. I was devastated.

Apparently, Stan's plane had been in a formation of thirty-six airplanes doing a troop drop at one of the drop zones near Fort Bragg. The formation leader, our group commander, was too late in starting the reduction of airspeed for the drop and then reduced power too rapidly. This caused the following squadron of nine airplanes to reduce power much more rapidly when they saw that they were closing in on the squadron ahead. When the next squadrons saw the compression, they had to pull off even more power to try to get back into position, causing an accordion effect that was hard to rectify.

Stan's plane had been in the last squadron. A pilot in the squadron ahead of him saw the danger of stalling out so he had applied power and pulled up out of formation. Unfortunately, his airplane had still been dropping troops and one of the paratroopers slammed into the windshield of Stan's plane, killing Stan and the paratrooper immediately. Other paratroopers got snagged on the wing and tail of Stan's plane and went down with the airplane as it crashed. Fortunately, all of the paratroopers who had been inside Stan's plane successfully jumped from the airplane before it crashed.

A contributing factor to this terrible crash was the design of the parachutes. The parachutes that the 82nd Airborne had at the time were called

T-7 chutes. When the chutes were opened by the static lines they popped open immediately. If the C-119 speed was too fast the chute could be damaged or the paratrooper could be injured so the planes had to slow down to 110 knots before the troops could jump. If the paratroopers were upside down when their chutes opened, they would be whipped upright and their mess kits and other attachments would go flying into the air.

In time, the Air Force developed a better chute called the T-10. This modified chute opened more gradually so troops could jump at a speed of about 125 knots instead of 110 knots. Not having to slow so drastically was much easier on the pilots and made flying formation for troop drops much safer.

BECAUSE I WAS FRESH OUT OF PILOT TRAINING, the various aircraft commanders I flew with hesitated to let me do much flying. I did fly some formation, and now and then I got a landing and takeoff, but I didn't get any formation takeoffs or landings. I flew most often with my squadron commander and while he was very generous with letting me do the flying, he still didn't give me any formation landings or takeoffs. I think most, if not all, the aircraft commanders did the formation takeoffs and landings because this was the most critical phase of the formation flights. I expected to spend my remaining three years of active duty as a co-pilot and did not expect to ever be checked out as an aircraft commander.

I had been at Charleston for about four months when at a morning briefing, the operations officer, Captain Red Nelson, said, "If any of you have any civilian time over 800 hp, bring your logbook in and we can put the time on your Form 5." When I brought my logbook to him he said, "Wow, we can check you out as an aircraft commander."

I thought, *Who, me?* Apparently, they were running short of qualified aircraft commanders at that time and the prospect of becoming one was very exciting to me. I expected the training to take a long time since I had done only a few landings and takeoffs in the C-119 and no formation landings or takeoffs. I had some training sessions with a designated instructor pilot that included simulated single engine operations, stalls, steep turns, landings, and takeoffs.

I had not done any formation takeoffs or formation landings during day or night when one day at the morning briefing I saw my name on the daily schedule listed as an aircraft commander for that day's recurrent nine-ship formation training. I was quite surprised. We were scheduled for four hours of day formation and were scheduled again that night for three hours of night formation. My co-pilot for the day had been checked out as an aircraft commander in Korea and had experience in formation takeoffs and landings. There were a few co-pilots like this in our squadron. During the Korean War, the requirement for aircraft commanders was 700 hours of total flight time instead of the 1,000 hours required in the states. Even so, I had about 1,700 hours of total flight time logged at this point including my civilian time, which was twice the amount my co-pilot had.

I did OK on the takeoff but when it came time to do the 360 overhead and formation landing, I was a little over my head. I got a little low on final and had to fight the controls a bit as I got into the wash from the airplane ahead. When I touched down, my feet were shaking so hard that it was difficult to use the brakes, so I had to use a lot of reverse to stop the plane. It was comforting to have someone experienced with formation landings and takeoffs in the right seat.

From that time on, I got the hang of it quite fast and I began to feel very comfortable about my ability to handle the airplane. I felt very confident about being an aircraft commander; it was not much different from when I soloed the B-25 in flight training. I just needed to get some exposure to doing the formation takeoffs and landings.

NOT TOO LONG AFTER I BECAME AN AIRCRAFT commander, a request came into the squadron from wing headquarters to supply a pilot and co-pilot to ferry a brand-new C-119G model from McClellan Air Force Base near Sacramento, California, to Japan. I volunteered for the trip. My co-pilot was from the 745th squadron at Charleston and he was a recent graduate from pilot training. We headed to Sewart Air Force Base near Nashville, Tennessee, where we were given some training in the G model, which was about the same as we had been flying except it had different propellers—Aeroproducts instead of Hamilton Standards. Then we proceeded to McClellan Air Force Base where we met up with our navigator and radio operator.

Our navigator turned out to be a captain in his forties who also had a commercial license. When we first met on the ramp by the C-119 that we were going to ferry, he appeared somewhat stunned. All he said was, "I'm not going." He immediately turned around and headed back into the hangar. He told his boss that he wasn't going to Japan with those kids out there. His boss told him that he was, indeed, going. He was not happy.

The trip involved five legs across the Pacific islands and by the time we reached Guam, the navigator was starting to relax and seemed to have much more confidence in us. During out last leg to Japan, however, I put this confidence to the test.

Just after we passed Tinian and Saipan, we received a radio message asking if we could stop at Iwo Jima to pick up an emergency appendicitis case. I told the radio operator to tell them we would stop. Our navigator said, "What? Don't you know that there is a typhoon there?" I said I did know about the typhoon but Iwo Jima was on the fringes of it and it was only blowing about 50 knots. He was not happy.

After breaking out of the overcast at Iwo Jima, I noticed that the waves were quite big. I lined up on final and let the airplane crab into the wind. I did not have the slightest concern about the crosswind because the C-119 can handle a lot of it and I had experienced more wind than this before. I thought I would wait until crossing the threshold to straighten it out. I lowered the left wing and pushed hard on the rudder to align with the runway just before touchdown.

Well, now is the time to talk a little about the pilot seat in a C-119. The seat was mounted on two sets of rails, with a lever on the seat that was used to move it back and to the left when getting in and out. A long pin through both sets of rails locked the seat in position. When I got into the seat at Guam, I let the pin fall into place with the help of a spring and I wiggled my seat to make sure it was locked, as I always did. But this was a new airplane so everything was a little tight and the pin did not go all the way down with spring power to securely lock the seat. I should have pushed down on the locking pin to make sure it was all the way down but I had never had to do that before.

So as we came in for a landing with the crosswind on Iwo Jima, I pushed hard on the rudder pedal to straighten the aircraft for touchdown. The resulting force on the seat popped out the locking pin and my seat shot back and to the left, yanking the controls from my hands at a critical moment. I immediately realized that drastic action was required. I unbuckled my seat belt, slid off the seat onto the floor, and mashed the right rudder with my foot. The nose swung back around and lined up with the runway just as we touched down. I could not initiate a go-around because I could not reach the throttles. Fortunately, I could see out the left side because the C-119 had additional windows just above the floor level to improve the view looking down. I could also reach the nose wheel steering lever that was now above my head. As I was lying on the cockpit floor with my headset askew and covering one of my eyes, I heard the tower say, "Nice landing." My co-pilot looked at me and said, "What are you doing down there?"

After we stopped, I scrambled back up on the seat and pulled it in place while thanking my co-pilot for all the help he did not give me. As I turned around to look at the navigator I was thinking he surely would be impressed at my ability to spring into action and complete the landing in a strong crosswind while sitting on the floor looking through one eye without the benefit of a windshield. Instead I found the navigator holding his shaking head in his hands. Instead of being impressed with my skills, I guess he thought that the airplane landed itself while I laid on the floor. I had a hard time getting him back in the airplane. We completed the rest of the trip without further stress on the navigator. After our takeoff from Iwo Jima on the ramp into the wind, I do remember him saying, "Nice takeoff." I think he was simply expressing his relief that maybe he was going to live through this trip after all.

We were supposed to bring a tired C-119 back to the States but after we landed at Ashiya, Japan, the navigator tore out of the airplane and came back to say that the return trip was cancelled. I had a pretty good idea why but I did not question it. I was the aircraft commander but the navigator's rank made him the mission commander. Since it was to be a tired C-119, I figured maybe the good Lord was looking after me. We instead rode back to the States on a Navy NATS C-118 flight.

I RETURNED TO MY SQUADRON IN CHARLESTON AND continued flying as a C-119 aircraft commander. We flew a variety of missions, generally supporting the 82nd Airborne training at Fort Bragg and hauling equipment and supplies to other bases, including Kindley Air Force Base in Bermuda. I flew every chance I got in order to gain more experience but also because I simply loved to fly. In addition to being able to check out airplanes on weekends for my requests, I was willing to fly co-pilot for other pilots on their flights on weekends. Some months I flew 140 hours or more.

At one point, the squadron deployed a few aircraft to San Juan, Puerto Rico, to haul hurricane relief supplies to a small airport in Haiti. The remote airport had a coral landing strip that was only about 3,000 feet long, as opposed to our usual landing strip length of 5,000 feet or more. This gave me an opportunity to practice my short field landings.

On another trip we flew to Ramie Air Force Base on the east side of Puerto Rico for some maneuvers. The B-36s, the largest long-range bombers in the Strategic Air Command, were based there at that time and I was very interested in seeing that operation. This was around the same time that Jimmy Stewart starred in the movie *Strategic Air Command*, flying a B-36. I would have loved to have been his co-pilot.

The wing commander at Charleston had a girlfriend in Texas and I found myself scheduled to fly with him on several trips to Brooks Air Force Base near San Antonio. We flew across the southern states at night and very often there were a lot of thunderstorms. We had no weather radar so we would simply try to pick a heading that would take us between the flashes of lightning, but that did not always work. A few times we thought we had it made when suddenly there was a big flash right in front of us just before we flew through a lot of hail. Given the sound the hail made on the plane, I was always sure there would be damage but surprisingly there never was.

On one flight from Texas back to Charleston, without the wing commander, we were flying along on a nice, sunny day when a Douglas A-26 went flying by our right wing with the left engine feathered. We decided he was not going to get away with that. Even though he had a faster airplane than we did, we had about 3,000 more horsepower than he did. I thought that maybe we could somehow show him that we also had a hot airplane. As he continued on ahead of us we saw him unfeather the engine and put it back in operation. I increased power to maximum continuous and we started gaining on him. I realized that I would need an altitude advantage so I started a gradual climb. It took a long time to get about 2,000 feet higher. About the time I was getting close to him, I put the airplane in a shallow dive and feathered the right engine just as we were about to pass him. The only problem was we never did pass him. As soon as he saw us he added power, feathered his left engine again, and pulled away from us at a rapid rate. We showed him all right. We showed him what a slow airplane we were flying.

PROBABLY HALF OF MY 2,000 HOURS OF C-119 flying was done in formation with anywhere between three and thirty-six planes; a good share of that was done at night. The night and day formation procedures were a carryover from World War II and were flown similar to fighter formations. The formation join-ups at night were much more difficult. Most of the pilots in the squadron hated night formation flying but I loved the challenge. At my age I thought I had nine lives. It was always exciting, sometimes a little too exciting.

I had two close calls during night formation, one just before I checked out as an aircraft commander and one after. The first close call came as I was flying co-pilot with Captain Tom Hoos in a thirty-six-airplane formation. We were set up to do an early morning flyby at Shaw Air Force Base near Columbia, South Carolina. This required a night takeoff and join-up at Charleston.

All airplanes got airborne in good order but shortly after takeoff, the squadron leader of the third squadron reported that he had lost sight of the first and second squadrons and was not able to join-up. The group leader replied, "Well, we will make a 360-degree turn so you can slide into position." I thought, *This is going to be interesting. Why doesn't he put one of the groups at different altitudes?*

Pretty soon some red passing lights started to show up on the horizon ahead. Then more appeared until there were red lights all across the horizon. The passing light is in the leading edge of each wing on military airplanes and shines a narrow beam straight out, so if you see the light, then that plane is headed right for you.

The rate of closure was so fast that, before anyone could maneuver, eighteen airplanes flew headlong through the other eighteen airplanes.

Planes were pulling up, diving, and turning sharply in every direction, resulting in thirty-six individual airplanes flying all over the area. We all set course for the airport and began to call the tower for landing instructions. The air was full of airplanes calling the tower all at the same time. The tower staff did their best for a while but they were soon overwhelmed and we stopped getting responses so we all started landing on our own. Somehow we all got down and there were no collisions.

After I was upgraded to aircraft commander, I was on a night training flight with just our squadron of nine airplanes. Our squadron commander had been trying to improve our competency for night formation so we had been doing these training flights for a few nights.

The formation configuration was called a V of Vs, with nine airplanes. I was in the number two position in the third element, which is on the left side of the lead element. The way it is supposed to work is the nine airplanes take off in ten-second intervals and after flying straight out for so many seconds, depending on your position, a 180-degree left turn with constant bank is initiated, and all airplanes are supposed to start their turn at a point that would slide all the airplanes into position upon completion of the turn.

Even though there were formation lights all across the top of each aircraft's wing, it is far more difficult to judge rate of closure at night without being able to see the outline of the airplane. My third element leader had been having trouble sliding into position by the completion of the turn. He was afraid of overshooting and colliding with the lead element. The squadron commander, Major James Hill, said that we were going to keep doing it until we got it right. After several nights, the squadron commander told my element leader that if he was not in position by the completion of the turn, he was going to replace him. I remember hoping that I wouldn't be the replacement. My element leader assured the squadron commander that he would indeed be in position.

So, that night as we started the left join-up turn, I instructed my co-pilot to keep an eye on the lead element and advise me how the join-up was going. I could not look that way because I was looking out my left side, flying right wing on the element leader. All of a sudden my co-pilot yelled, "Pull up! Pull up!" I took a quick look out his window and saw all kinds of lights closing fast. I immediately hauled back on the wheel as I heard and saw the three ships in the lead element pass underneath me, between me and the lead airplane that I was flying wing on. The number three airplane on the left side of our element dove for the ground. Again, the whole squadron was scattered and we flew individually back to the base.

Even with these close calls, I still loved doing the night formation training. Once at a briefing, the group commander, Colonel Bogue, said, "Last week I witnessed one of our youngest pilots do one of the finest night join-ups that I have ever seen, so don't tell me it can't be done." After the briefing, my squadron commander, Major Hill, came to me and said, "You know who he was talking about, don't you?" I said that I had an idea. He seemed to be very pleased, but what they did not realize was that the join-up they were referring to was a lot of luck. (Oh, maybe a little skill.)

That particular join-up happened at Farmington, New Mexico, after we had flown out a replacement engine for a C-119 that had lost an engine. I was to take the trip but Colonel Bogue decided he also wanted to go. I was amazed that we were able to get the engine changed in one day because a couple of months earlier I had seen a change like this take a week under my command as a second lieutenant. It is incredible what rank can do in the military. The engine change was finished up after dark so we launched the two airplanes for the return to Charleston, requiring a night join-up. The colonel had me in the left seat and I worked very hard to do it right. Thankfully, the join-up went smoothly and I earned some points in the colonel's mind.

Taken at Adak, Alaska, waiting for the headwinds to die down below 30 knots before departing for Misawa, Japan. From left to right, me, aircraft commander; Ed Schmalzried, pilot; Bill Anderson, co-pilot; and Al Uyechi, navigator.

Training in the North American B-25 at Reese Air Force Base, Lubbock, Texas.

Above: Head shot of me as an Air Force pilot.

Left: Visiting retired Colonel Bernt Balchen, famous Arctic pilot and family friend, in New York, 1954.

One of the primary cadets violating regulations in primary training by colliding with a cactus. He and another cadet were trying to outdo one another doing slow rolls near the ground. This fellow misjudged and collided with a cactus, knocking five feet off the right wing but managing to keep it in the air until he made a belly landing back at Marana, Arizona.

After being released from the Air Force in 1956, I flew the DC-3 for a couple of years before switching to the C-46, shown on page 72.

The C-119 assigned to me during operation Genetrix.

This is a picture of me taken shortly after being promoted to instructor pilot in the USAF C-119.

C-46 on the Chandalar Lake ice delivering mining equipment. This is the same C-46 retrieved from the ice earlier.

The first summer I flew captain on the DC-3. This photo was taken at Fort Yukon, Alaska, 1956.

Richard standing near the C-46 that landed too late on Peters Lake in the spring of 1958. The airplane was eventually retrieved and continued service for many years.

Twenty years before the Wien C-46 went through the ice at Peters Lake, my dad's Ford Tri-Motor went through the ice at Harding Lake in 1938. The plane was successfully retrieved.

6

Special Assignments

By 1955 I was designated as an instructor pilot and usually flew with a three-pilot crew. I had managed to get a friend from primary training, Ed Schmalzried, assigned with me to the 746th Troop Carrier Squadron and eventually he was assigned to my crew full-time along with pilot Bill Anderson. The three of us worked very well together.

In January 1955 we were assigned to participate in a massive training maneuver called Operation Snowbird. The goal of the maneuver was to practice deploying a large amount of troops and equipment between Sewart Air Force Base in Nashville, Tennessee, and Elmendorf Air Force Base in Anchorage, Alaska. The mission for the Charleston aircraft was to support the Sewart airplanes with parts and maintenance people. The primary mission was assigned to the wing at Sewart Air Force Base in Nashville, Tennessee, and our wing was assigned to support them.

We spent the first night of our mission at Sewart, sleeping in some World War II–era, two-story barracks. During the night, the barracks next to ours caught fire. Personnel came through our barracks to wake everyone up, yelling for us to evacuate the building. There was a lot of noise and sirens and we had to stand outside our barracks until it was determined that it was safe to go back inside for the night. In the morning, we had a hard time waking Ed up but we finally managed it and left the barracks to go to breakfast.

As we walked out Ed exclaimed, "Holy cow! What happened here?" We then realized that Ed had slept through all the commotion; we hadn't noticed that he hadn't been with us outside.

Over the next two days we flew to Great Falls, Montana, and then on to Fort Nelson, British Columbia, where the overnight temperature was about thirty degrees below zero. Because we didn't have engine heaters, we were told to use our oil dilution systems for a certain amount of time, depending on air temperature. When I flew for Wien Airlines, I had learned that if you dilute the oil with gasoline it washes out sludge from the engine, which clogs the oil screens with the resulting loss of oil pressure on engines that are not low on time since overhaul. We eventually deactivated the oil dilution for that reason. Before that, we diluted even in the summer to keep the engines desludged.

At Fort Nelson, I elected to use the dilution system for only about a minute or so, just to dilute the oil in the oil lines and not in the oil tank. On the inside of the fuselage of the C-119s there were eight gas heaters, which could be directed to different parts of the airplane, such as the cockpit, windshield, and the cargo compartment, and could also be used as wing anti-ice heat and engine accessory heat. I was able to find some covers for the engine and I directed the aircraft heaters to the accessory section, hoping that enough heat would get to the power section of the engines to permit a start. The engines did start but the oil pressure pegged out on the high side, so I kept the rpm as low as I could until the oil pressures started to come down. I suspect other pilots were using the recommended time for oil dilution, so several aircraft were grounded with engine changes. As a result, after completing the trip between Anchorage and Charleston, I was sent back for another round-trip to Alaska. I used this oil dilution technique on all cold weather stops and I think that I was the only airplane that completed two round-trips. I did them both in about two weeks, which was very strenuous given that I flew about 120 hours during that time.

Because we flew at around 10,000 feet most of the time, I quickly learned how important it was to use oxygen. I had never flown so many hours in such a short time at that altitude without supplemental oxygen and so I did not realize how important it was to eat and to drink plenty of water. I ended up catching a bad cold and losing about fifteen pounds by the time I returned to Charleston. I was very anxious for the flight surgeon to ground me in Charleston so I could rest up and I was surprised when he didn't. If he had known how eager I was to fly any time I could, he might have realized that I really was exhausted.

After that experience, I always made sure I had plenty of food and water and I used quite a bit of oxygen on long trips. I devised a procedure to heat canned food by placing it on top of the Aldis lamp (a powerful spotlight) so we could have hot food. It made a big difference in fatigue levels for me and my crews on long flights.

Not long after Operation Snowbird, we were told that the Troop Carrier Wing at Charleston had been assigned a special mission that would require extensive training. My first thought was that they would probably recruit the most experienced instructor pilots as aircraft commanders for this operation and I would probably be back to co-pilot if not reassigned to another squadron. After all, I was still just a second lieutenant. I soon found out that I had been selected as one of the aircraft commanders. Someone told me that I was the youngest instructor pilot in all of the 18th Air Force.

Initially, we were told very little about the mission. We began extensive local training in instrument approaches, single engine training, and overall precision flying. Many new navigators were assigned to the squadrons, most of them just out of navigator school. In order to give the navigators sufficient training for this operation, we made many fifteen-hour-plus flights over water.

By this time I was living off base. One night, my good friend and fellow aircraft commander, Lieutenant "Square Deal" McNeal, was assigned to take a trip. His airplane did not check out so they gave him my airplane, 518165. Both engines quit on takeoff and the plane crashed about a block away from where I was living, killing Square, his co-pilot, and two other crew members. There were two survivors but they were badly injured. I heard many sirens during the night but did not know what happened until I reported to the base the next morning. Square's death hit me hard. He was very entertaining and every time he began to tell a story, I started laughing even before I knew what he was going to say.

Because both engines had quit, sabotage was suspected; however, the investigation revealed that it was caused by human error, not sabotage. When my airplane had been serviced, the ground crew was checking out a new man on how to refuel and service the airplane. Apparently, the new guy put gasoline in the tank that held the water methanol for the water injection system. Water injection was used to achieve maximum power for takeoff with heavy loads. When the system was activated during takeoff, the engines lost power shortly after liftoff. This would no doubt have happened to me the next time I flew the airplane. I guess God was looking after me that night.

Our preparations for the mission continued, though we still hadn't been informed of the details. I made several trips to Hagerstown, Maryland, delivering airplanes to be modified for the mission and bringing them back after the modifications were completed. Sometimes I was a passenger among a load of pilots who would be flying the modified planes back to Charleston. On one flight, we pilots were harassing the pilot in command by walking back and forth together in the cargo compartment, constantly changing the weight distribution so he had to keep trimming the airplane. At one point, about six of us were standing in the rear clamshell doors. I happened to notice there were only four small bolts holding the doors on the airplane. I pointed this out to my fellow aviators and there was a big scramble to move off the doors. I guess the joke would have been on us if we departed the airplane without our chutes on.

During the modifications on each plane in Maryland, the clamshell doors on the rear of the fuselage were replaced with a shape that looked like the trailing edge of a fat wing. The modified rear end was called a beaver tail. With the flip of a switch in the cockpit, the bottom of the beaver tail, which was hinged on the trailing edge, would hydraulically move up to the top of the beaver tail. The beaver tail was hinged to the fuselage on the top, and while the bottom was moving up, the rest of the assembly moved up also, allowing the whole rear end to be wide open.

A hydraulically operated pole assembly was attached to the floor on each side at the rear of the cargo compartment. The poles were stored in the cargo area at a forward location until they were inserted into the hydraulically operated assemblies by two crew members on each side. This assembly was designed to be operated by five men—a winch operator and four pole handlers. Two men on each side would handle the poles as they were fed into an assembly that would hydraulically move the poles down on each side with rope and hooks attached in three places, one on the bottom of the poles and one in the middle of the loop between the two poles. The poles were about thirty-four feet long and extended down about fifty-eight degrees. The cargo compartment was modified to carry an additional 1,000 gallons of fuel, bringing the total to 3,500 gallons.

When the time came to actually start the specific mission training, we found out what the program was all about—taking pictures of Russia. High altitude balloons with newly developed camera equipment were being launched in some neutral European countries, such as Turkey and Germany. The balloons were designed to drift in the jet stream over Russia and when the balloons reached the Pacific it would be our job to recover them either in the air or from the water, if we were unable to catch them in the air. All personnel involved in the recovery operation—called Genetrix—had to have a top secret clearance. My friends and family in Fairbanks were wondering why the FBI was there asking so many questions about me.

Initially it was top secret but it was eventually declassified. Much has been said about the U-2 program and the later SR-71 Blackbird operations and satellite surveillance, but I have never heard anything about the balloon recovery operation. Even though it was stone age technology compared to the SR-71 operation, it actually marked the beginning of spying technology during the Cold War.

For our training, a C-119 with a crew on oxygen launched loads at about 20,000 feet. In each load, there were four 24-foot chutes that deployed with a 105-foot line extended above, attached to a small, reinforced nylon web drogue chute. The beaver tail was hydraulically opened and the poles were inserted into the hydraulic assemblies by the four pole handlers who were attached to the plane with safety lines, and then the poles were hydraulically tilted down about fifty degrees. Flying at around 15,000 feet, we began making passes, trying to capture the chutes.

It was necessary to make contact with the drogue chute at a low airspeed, about 115 knots, so as not to tear the rope lines apart; at the same time, we had to descend about 1,200 feet per minute. This required the props to be set at a high rpm with a low power setting so the props could create enough drag. The combination of high rpm and low manifold pressure was very hard on the engines. When the propeller was driving the engines, instead of the other way around, the crankshaft was not getting the oil pressure and lubrication where it was needed and we had some engine failures. We were told to reduce rpm to be more compatible with the low manifold pressure, but this did not give us enough drag to keep the airspeed down on contact with the drogue chute. When we tried this, the higher contact speed caused the rigging on the chutes to be ripped apart and we lost some recoveries. We knew that putting the landing gear down would help, but we did not want the chute to get tangled up in the gear. We just had to abuse the engines with higher rpm to make a successful recovery.

After I finished my training and qualification, I was made an instructor to check out other pilots. My first candidate was a captain who was about forty years old and a World War II bomber veteran. He had a wife and several children and apparently did not feel that he had nine lives, as I did. It was difficult for me to get him to cut the time down on his passes in order to get as many shots at the chutes as possible before they hit the water. After missing a pass, we would go out about ten seconds and then make the sharpest possible turn back toward the chutes. I tried to get him to turn sharper but he didn't like to feel the ailerons bucking in his hands because part of the wing was stalling and burbling over the ailerons. He kept yelling that we were going to stall, but I knew the airplane could handle a steeper bank at that low airspeed.

After making a successful catch on one of the training periods, he decided to go back to the cargo compartment and watch how the rear crew winched in the load. During the process I heard a noise and felt a jolt. The captain soon returned to the cockpit and I noticed that a lot of his hair was ripped off one side of his head and he had some bloody scratches on his scalp. It turned out that a new winch operator had threaded the cable incorrectly, causing a cable deflector to fail. The cable snapped and the frayed end went flying wildly through the compartment, swiping the captain's head.

The next day, with the captain's head freshly bandaged, we went up again. The day was quite smoky, which made it very difficult to make the catch. Under normal conditions, in order to verify that you were flying directly toward the chute, you had to make sure that the chute was absolutely stationary against the background. But on this day, we couldn't even see any background. The captain was not having any luck and kept missing the chutes. We had one more shot before it hit the water and I said, "Let me see if I can snag it so we can at least log a recovery for the rear end crew." I had to work at it with the rudders but I made the contact. It looked like everything was going to be fine as we leveled off and added power. All of a sudden the nose pitched up, the control wheel came back toward me, and we stalled. I tried to lower the nose and recover from the stall but my knees were trapped by the control wheel and I could not use the rudders. I had to use differential power on the engines to keep the wings as level as I could.

While I was fighting for our lives, the captain was screaming loudly, which was very unnerving. I put the flaps down but that did not seem to help and I was sure we were going to die. I saw no way out but I was not going to give up. I had heard that in situations like this your whole life flashes before you. I can now verify that that is the case and I do know what it feels like just before you know you are going to die. Fortunately I was not able to keep the airplane right side up and it rolled over partially inverted. This caused the airspeed to increase when the airplane was diving rapidly toward the water. Suddenly, I was able to lower the nose and I regained flying speed.

Later, I figured out what caused the pitch up. I had been a little low on contact with the drogue chute and instead of the chute getting caught by the hooks, the loop between the poles caught the line below the drogue chute. The chute remained inflated and acted like a kite, pulling the cable higher and higher until it touched the elevator. When that happened, the elevator went up and the control wheel came back into my stomach, trapping my knees. The more the nose went up, the more the elevator laid on the cable. I recently saw a picture of a C-119 snagging the chute and I noticed that the rigging had been modified to include another loop with hooks a few feet up to prevent the drogue chute from inflating in a similar circumstance.

On the control wheel there were several buttons. One of them was a cable cutter button to be used in case anything went wrong during the recovery. Early in my training, I had inadvertently pushed this button while wrestling with the control wheel during a turn back to the chutes. My squadron commander was not happy. Not wanting another scolding, I had worked out a system with my winch operator whereby he could use a switch near his seat to deactivate my button on the wheel but could reactivate it quickly if I called back to him. He could also flip his cable cutter switch if he saw a problem (which he should have done before the cable touched the elevator) and if that failed he could use a big manual cable cutter. During the stall, I pushed all the buttons on the wheel as I screamed at him into the interphone to cut the cable. The winch operator fired the cable cutter but it cut only partway through the cable. He was not able to use the manual cutter because he and the rest of the crew were all being thrown around in the back and he could not reach it in time. The cable was stretched across the cutting ram and by the time it hit the backstop, most of the energy from the fired chisel was absorbed by the tension of the cable tightened by the still inflated drogue chute. When the airplane did a partial split S, the additional pull was enough to finish severing the cable. We recovered immediately, but not very high above the waves.

After my inadvertent cutting of the cable during my training and to stop the work-around of disarming the pilot's button, a cup was engineered around the button so you had to stick your thumb in to push it. If the palm of your hand slid over the guarded button, it would not cut the cable. It seems that the modifications that were made were a result of things that I experienced. I wondered, *Why did all these things have to happen to me?*

After we recovered from the stall, I flew the airplane back to Charleston in the right seat. The captain was in shock. I got out of the airplane and walked to our operations building. It wasn't long before I started to fall apart. During the emergency all I could think about was how to get out of the situation but now that it was over, I began to think that I would probably never want to fly again. I looked out at the airplane and the captain was still sitting in the seat.

During my debriefing with the group commander, I stretched the truth and said I was fine. I wasn't fine, really, but it didn't take long before I was fully operational again. I recovered but that near-death experience stayed with me. To this day, I think of every day that I am still alive as a bonus. I learned to be thankful for all the wonderful events and great family life that I have been blessed with. It truly was a life changing experience.

Even though I returned to flying, for the first time I was aware that someday I might get killed doing it, which marked a significant turning point in my life. I had already lost several friends in crashes and I had certainly seen others walk away from flying after having bad experiences. I remembered a young, very sharp first lieutenant aircraft commander who had experienced complete electrical failure and lost all his flight instruments while in the clouds. He ended up diving out of the clouds and barely missed the ground. I was in operations when he came in and threw his wings on the operations officer's desk saying that he was never going to fly again. Even with my near-death experience, I knew flying was my life and I would not be able to just walk away from it but I was sure happy to be alive.

Every pilot is different, though. My experience with the captain, and with several others later on, got me thinking about how the Air Force or airlines evaluated pilot candidates. It is very difficult to know how a pilot will react in a true emergency. You can train to handle emergencies but in those circumstances, the emergency is not real and the fear of dying is not present. I have flown with pilots who do a great job flying the airplane and show good judgment but if a bad situation develops and the outcome is questionable, panic engulfs them and they can no longer function. I will never forget the screaming of the captain as I was trying to recover from the stall. I sure could have used his help but he was a distraction. I was glad to find out that my survival instinct overshadowed any performance deficiencies during an emergency.

WE FINISHED THE AIR RECOVERY PART OF THE training and moved onto the next phase, which was to qualify for water recovery. If the camera equipment ended up in the water, a chemically activated telescoping pole with a large hook on the end would extend upward from the floating package. The rigging on the airplane remained the same but the hooks were removed from the end of the poles and in the middle of the loop. The loop between the poles caught the hook on the top of the telescoping pole on the floating camera package.

The training was moved to Lake Moultrie, not too far from Charleston. We practiced with packages both in the water and on land. This exercise required excellent depth perception so the loop strung between the poles, about forty feet below the cockpit level, would contact the poles on the package within a foot or two below the hook on the top of the poles. If you misjudged the altitude, you either missed the telescoping pole or you drove the poles from the airplane into the water. If the poles broke, sometimes the pieces ended up hitting the elevator. When we practiced at our deployment station, we found out the large waves in the open sea made it especially difficult.

It was necessary to make the pass at just the right altitude and airspeed and rotate at just the right time to catch the hook and be able to lift the package out of the water without letting it settle back in, which could damage the camera equipment. After catching the hook, the pilot had to pull back on the control wheel to start a steep climb of about thirty-five degrees, calling for max power at the same time. The co-pilot would slam the prop control full forward and advance throttles to max power. The airspeed was quite low to begin with and then we had to level off at about 1,000 feet just above stall speed. This was a very hairy operation and I wondered how it would work in rough seas.

Our training complete, the three Charleston squadrons were divided up into six detachments. I ended up in the 746th squadron and was slated to go to Kodiak Naval Air Station, Alaska, which pleased me because it was close to home. The 746th detachment went to Adak, Alaska, and the other four squadrons were based at Misawa, Johnson (near Tokyo), Itazuke, and Okinawa air bases in Japan. This effectively created a net of recovery aircraft, depending on where the winds took the balloons. In October 1955 we packed up and headed for our assignments.

At Kodiak, we continued to practice the water pickups. The Navy helped by providing a seagoing tug to deposit a simulated package out in the bay. I was in the first group of five airplanes that were scheduled for this training. When the tug was in position and the package was placed in the water, we started to make our runs. I was disappointed that I was the last airplane in line to try for the pickup because I thought the first plane would be able to snag it on the first pass. If an airplane did not make the pickup they were supposed to mark the spot with a smoke bomb. I knew from our radio contact that the first four planes had missed the package but they didn't drop any smoke bombs so I wasn't able to see it in time to make the pickup. I spotted it and was able to overfly with some skidding and drop our smoke bomb. Once the object was marked, I figured the next plane to try again would manage to do the recovery. As it turned out, none of the other four planes that had circled back to try again managed to see it in time to snag it.

When I saw it on my next pass, I had to do a sharp turn to get to it. The waves were quite high and I knew it was going to be a challenge. As I approached the package, I tried to determine whether the bundle was going to be on the top of a wave or in a trough. It looked like the package was going to be in a trough so, not wanting to bust my poles on the top of a wave, I waited until the last second and then made an abrupt rotation, pitching the airplane up to deflect the poles down into the trough. Voila. We got it. I admit it was a lot of luck, but even so, my squadron commander was very impressed.

EVEN THOUGH ONE AIRCRAFT FROM KODIAK SNAGGED A balloon in northern Alaska, it soon became obvious that most of the balloons were drifting over Japan, not toward Alaska. In January 1956, two airplanes from Kodiak and two from Adak were sent to Tokyo to reinforce the recovery capability in that area. Captain Stan Broderick and I were selected to go from Kodiak. Before we left, we were each encouraged to put a name on our aircraft. Stan named his "Stanley Steamer." My crew wanted me to put "Merrill's Marauder" on our ship, based on the famous colonel in the China-Burma theater in World War II. I thought that might be a little too egotistical, so we named it "Arctic Angel."

When we departed for Japan, we were required to wear Mark IV exposure suits in case we had to ditch in the cold water. The early legs of the journey went fine but on our last leg, as we headed for Misawa, Japan, we found that the headwinds were higher than forecast. Our navigator, Lieutenant Uyechi, kept a close eye on our speed and as long as it looked like we would still have enough fuel to go to our alternate, Tokyo, we continued. By the time we got to our equal time point (decision time), it looked like our alternate fuel would be questionable. We elected to continue because the Misawa weather was holding; however, we soon received a report that Misawa had dropped to 300 feet and one-quarter-mile visibility. We began to think that we should have turned around when we had the chance but now we were committed. The stress and sweat factors were rising.

Speaking of sweat, we had been wearing the Mark IV exposure suits ever since leaving Adak with an emergency vest on top of the exposure suit and a life vest over that. Body moisture was accumulating in the insulated underwear under my rubber suit, the tight rubber collar was chafing my neck, and our butts were getting very sore from sitting on the hard dinghy attached to the bottom of our chutes.

With our three-pilot crew, one of us could get some rest by lying on top of the auxiliary fuel tanks. I was lying on the tanks with my headset on when I heard Ed Schmalzried say on the interphone, "What did he say? We have crossed the line and are too close to Russia?" I came flying off the tanks and raced to the cockpit.

The last thing we wanted was to be caught in Russian airspace with all that secret equipment onboard. That probably would have ended the mission and maybe ended us. We had not been told that our wing commander, Colonel Daniels, had created a buffer line we were not supposed to cross, which he dubbed the "Daniel line." We had crossed the Daniel line but had not actually crossed the Russian border so the situation was not as bad as we initially thought. We did, however, make a sharp turn away from the border.

About an hour later, when it was my turn on the flight deck, I noticed that there was quite a bit of Saint Elmo's fire dancing around the propellers. I had seen this several times before but had always heard that it was harmless. It was fun to watch. Since it was dark, I soon saw it in front of the windshield looking like headlights extending out from the pitot tubes. I had my head up against the windshield when there was a loud bang and a blinding flash of light. It sounded like someone had pulled the trigger on a Colt 45 right in front of my face. Everyone in the cockpit was temporarily blinded. I was hand flying the plane at the time, so I reached for the autopilot button on the center console. From the right seat, Bill Anderson was shaking my shoulder and yelling at me, "Are you all right?" Because he was shaking me, I was having trouble finding the autopilot-engage button. I finally had to shout, "Yes, I am all right!"

What had happened was that we had been flying in the clouds for most of the trip, allowing static electricity to build up on the airplane, causing the Saint Elmo's display. The buildup was so great that it actually created a bolt of lightning from the airplane.

In a few moments, our sight started to return and we saw smoke and flames coming from the electronics area. The operations officer and the crew chief scooted up to the A deck and started grabbing armloads of wiring. Maybe the fire extinguisher would have been a better plan because we soon found out that we had no more Loran for navigation and that we had lost the HF radio, which was our last communications capability we had on the airplane. We had left Kodiak with our UHF radios inoperative because the radio department was unable to fix a problem with them by the time we were scheduled to depart. The two VHF antennas had been converted to receive and home in on the balloons with a direction finder. They were much thinner and not as strong as the original antennas and so when they iced up during the flight, they broke off, which then eliminated the use of the VHF radios.

As we approached within VHF radio contact, we dialed in the ground control intercept (GCI) frequency, 134.1, on our VOR navigation radios.

Fortunately, the military navigation frequencies went up into the communication radio frequency range. Civilian navigational radios did not do this. We were hoping that when the GCI picked us up on their radar, they would give us a call. Sure enough, when we got within range they started calling us but we could not respond. Eventually they said, "If you read us, turn left to such and such heading." I immediately turned to that heading and they acknowledged the turn. What a relief. As we got closer they turned us over to the ground-controlled approach (GCA) frequency. After GCA gave us a few heading and altitude changes, they turned us over to the final controller. The weather that GCA gave us was about 100 feet and one-eighth-mile visibility. As we slid down the glide slope, we unexpectedly got a view of the runway lights. I thought the landing should be no sweat. But then the lights quickly disappeared. We broke out about 200 feet but as soon as we touched down, we went into a solid wall of blowing snow. I immediately went into reverse thrust and used the brakes hard while trying to maintain runway heading. When we stopped, I did not try to taxi because visibility was zero. As we were waiting for a follow-me vehicle, the runway lights started to appear. I started taxiing and met the follow-me about halfway to the ramp. After a fifteen-hour flight and spending about twenty-two hours in the exposure suits, we were very happy to be on the ground.

When I arrived at the BOQ I got out of the suit and took a welcome shower. I expected that I would probably fall right to sleep after hitting the bed but I was so wired I could not sleep for hours. I kept reliving the flight.

The second lieutenant who flew with me to Japan on the ferry flight was the communications officer there. At the base in Misawa, they were able to repair all the electronic damage, except for the UHF radio, in about two days. When I first walked around the airplane in daylight, I was surprised to see that the nose cap was pushed in and the right forward part of the fuselage from the nose cap back about six feet was buckled in between the formers.

WHEN THE WEATHER IMPROVED WE WENT ON TO Johnson Air Force Base near Tokyo where we were placed on standby and alert status. Most of the balloons were being snatched from the stations to the south. One captain was getting most of them and he received the Distinguished Flying Cross for it.

I flew only one recovery mission in the company of another airplane while in Japan. The other airplane was commanded by Captain Harold "Slick" Bierman, one of the airplanes from Adak. We were given headings to intercept the balloon. We had onboard what looked like the old rotary dial on a telephone so when we got close, we dialed a number to activate the homing transmitter mounted on the camera unit so our automatic direction finder (ADF) could point to the balloon. When we had it in sight, we could then dial another number to explode the balloon and allow the parachutes to descend.

Captain Bierman's airplane was number one for the recovery. We headed directly for it and the control center in Japan said, "You should be able to see it now."

Captain Bierman said he did not see it yet. I told our radio operator to tell Japan that we saw it. They said, "OK, you take the number one position."

I was just about to dial it down when Captain Bierman said he saw it so they reassigned him number one position. I thought, *Darn, maybe he will miss it and I will be right behind him for the catch.* No such luck. He got it.

By this time the balloon launches were winding down so we were sent back to Kodiak. Several of the balloons had come down in Russia. The Russians were told that they were weather balloons being used to study wind and jet streams at higher altitudes, but they didn't buy it. So by the time we arrived in Kodiak in March 1956, the Russians had raised such a fuss about the balloons that President Eisenhower had to shut Genetrix down. Coincidentally, as the military tracked the balloons across Europe and Russia, they actually did learn a lot about winds at higher elevations.

The word was out that when the mission was complete, the squadron would be disbanded and personnel would be reassigned to other units. I had been trying to arrange for my transfer to Air Rescue in Alaska ever since I was assigned to Troop Carrier in Charleston. I thought that this would be my opportunity to finish out my time in Air Rescue. I figured I would enjoy rescue flying with the extra bonus that I would be stationed near home. I had already begun working with our personnel officer to get the transfer when I found out that anyone with less than six months remaining in the service would be discharged at the port of entry, Seattle. I told the personnel officer to forget my request. He said, "Too late. I already have your orders for the 74th Air Rescue in Fairbanks." Boy, did I outsmart myself. The rest of my crew was discharged six months before I was.

When I was released from the C-119 squadron, my commanders lectured me never to talk about what we did. I kept that commitment until recently, when I heard that the program had been declassified and it is now public information on the Internet.

During Operation Genetrix about 480 balloons were launched but only about 44 capsules were recovered. The balloons photographed only about 10 percent of the Soviet Union, but the military still acquired some valuable information. By the time Genetrix ended, the U-2 spy plane was almost ready for operation and a new era of Cold War spying was about to begin.

ON MAY 6, THE ORDERS FOR THE TRANSFER of all personnel from Kodiak were ready to be picked up at Adak. Since there was a big termination party going on, our squadron commander, Major Hill, assigned us the job of flying to Adak that night, since my crew was the only crew that had not yet indulged in attitude adjustments.

Ed Schmalzried went with me but Bill Anderson and Al Uyechi stayed at Kodiak so we had a different navigator. We had been in the air about two hours when we started to lose altitude. I increased to climb power and we were able to maintain altitude for a short time but then we started to sink again. I went to maximum continuous power but we were still going down about 2,000 feet a minute. We had a radio altimeter that showed us closing with the mountains so I decided to turn around. As I started the turn, the rate of climb began to level off and soon we were climbing at about 2,000 feet a minute, so I continued on course and eased the power way back. I was very relieved but my relief did not last. Soon we began to get into some turbulence, which became severe. Ed was on the controls with me trying to help keep the airplane right side up. The sheer vertical currents were whipping the control wheel left and right and out of our hands.

The panel was moving all over the place making the instruments hard to read. We were trying to keep the airspeed between 50 and 150 knots but the airspeed indicator was hard to focus on. Fortunately, the directional gyro was a bigger instrument and the dial was set so the desired heading needle was straight up. I couldn't read the degrees but I managed to work the needle so it was pointing straight down, allowing us to reverse course. I did not feel that the twin boom configuration was as strong as most cargo designs because I had seen the booms from the cargo compartment bouncing up and down in light turbulence. My thought was that I would feather the engines at the first indication of structural failure after giving the bail out command. Fortunately the airplane held together. It wasn't long before we were in smooth air again. We flew that course for a while and then turned north in hopes of getting around the violent currents. When we thought we were far enough north, we set course again for Adak. The rest of the trip out and back was uneventful.

We later found out that area on the Aleutian chain develops a mountain wave from time to time. A mountain wave creates a rotor, which causes strong vertical currents and turbulence. Years later, a Wien Consolidated Airlines Fairchild F-27 hit a mountain wave while descending in to Iliamna and the wings snapped off, killing all onboard.

As part of the 74th Air Rescue squadron, I soon found myself back at Ladd Field where I had enlisted almost five years earlier. Because I had less than six months left in the service, they did not consider it worthwhile to send me to Fort Lauderdale to qualify as an aircraft commander so I was assigned as a co-pilot with a pilot and navigator on the SA-16 Albatross.

The keel on the SA-16 Albatross had a retractable runner that acted like a big ski and smaller skis were attached to the bottom of the wing floats. When I started flying on some missions with my pilot, I realized that he did not have a good feel for the aircraft. We went to Minchumina once and he was afraid to land because the strip was only about 4,000 feet long. He let me show him how it could be landed in half that distance.

Another time we were assigned a flight to Mount McKinley to do an airdrop on the Muldrow Glacier for a British mountain climbing expedition. As we approached the mountain, the pilot flew up the middle of the glacier valley. I thought, *OK, now let's move over to the right side so we will have room to turn around.*

He just kept flying straight ahead and when I looked at him I saw sweat running off his head. I could see that he was planning to fly to the upper end of the glacier and go over the top of the call. That wasn't going to work for me because I could see that we were slightly below the ridge of the call and blowing snow was coming over the ridge toward us. I grabbed the controls and said, "What are you doing?"

He immediately took his hands off the wheel. I then pulled the power off, veered over to the right side, and then banked left to make a pass down-glacier over the climbing party. I noted the altitude at their location and then pulled up to make a left pattern back for the drop. When flying up a glacier, you have to make sure you have enough altitude to make the turn. You might find the airspeed dropping off fast because you are climbing while thinking that you are flying level. We planted the load next to them and made a couple more passes to dump the rest.

Since then I have learned that there are many pilots who have no idea how much room there is between the airplane and a mountain. Granted, Mount McKinley (now Denali) is awesome and intimidating and it looks like you are about to hit it when you are actually a long way from it.

MY LAST SIX MONTHS IN THE AIR FORCE as part of the 74th Air Rescue squadron at Ladd Field in Fairbanks were unfulfilling and disappointing. I had looked forward to working in Air Rescue but it did not take long before I became disenchanted with the operation. I spent long hours on alert or standby, just sitting or sleeping at the base. This really drove me nuts because whenever I could get some time off, the airline had a trip for me. I passed my airline transport written exam and completed my check ride for my ATR and type rating for the DC-3.

The squadron had a number of Grumman SA-16 Albatrosses, a DC-4, and several helicopters. The SA-16s were triphibians, that is, they could land in the water, on land, or on snow. You would think that this combination of aircraft would have allowed us to do some serious rescuing. However, the pilots were having too many accidents so the command discontinued any snow operations and open sea water landings, approving only the two largest lakes in Alaska for water operation. They later approved Chandler Lake in the Brooks Range so some generals could go hunting and fishing. The only real rescue aircraft that we had were the helicopters, but an SA-16 or a DC-4 had to escort them wherever they went. I could not understand why the pilots were not better trained to be able to take advantage of the performance capabilities of the airplane, nor why they rotated pilots out of Alaska after two years, just as they were getting to know the country. When I was finally discharged in September 1956, I was more than ready to be out of the military.

7

A Civilian Again

Now that I was a civilian again, I plunged into flying for Wien Airlines and returned to college at the University of Alaska. I had considered returning to Pan American but when I looked at what my seniority number was there, I knew that it would be many years before I would ever be a captain. Also in Wien's favor was the fact that the flying in Alaska was far more interesting than the long overseas flights with few landings that I would be doing with Pan Am. The decision was made.

I was very happy to be out of the Air Force. I felt so lucky that I had a career that I loved and I couldn't believe that I was being paid to fly airplanes. I went to the airport every day, hoping to be on the next day's schedule. When I returned to Wien, having held a seniority position since 1950, I slid right into a captain's position ahead of some co-pilots who were World War II veterans and much older than I was. I definitely felt some animosity about that although I had earned my position through seniority and not because I was a Wien.

I suppose my name did catch some attention, however. Once, after checking out as captain in the DC-3, I was sitting in the restaurant in the Fairbanks terminal having breakfast one day without my cap and jacket. I overheard a passenger, when she heard that the captain's name was Wien, say, "I hope that he did not become a captain due to his name instead of his qualifications." This didn't bother me but I can understand why she might have thought that.

I enjoyed flying the DC-3 and learned it was capable of landing on much shorter runways than were normally used for it. One of my co-pilots, Frank Gregory, said that when he was flying for Interior Airways, he flew a lot with Bob Rice. I had known Bob Rice since I was a teenager when he was chief pilot for Wien Airlines. Bob had a reputation for being able to do the impossible with the DC-3 and the C-46. Frank told me that Bob used to land on the 700-foot intermediate Distant Early Warning (DEW) Line sights on the north coast that were built for smaller airplanes, such as the Cessna 180. This really intrigued me. One day I asked Bob how he did this. He spent quite a bit of time talking to me about how it was done. When I was scheduled to fly some trips to smaller airports at places like Bettles, Alatna, Hughes, and Hog River along the Koyukuk River I gradually experimented with his technique. I would pick a spot about 500 feet down the runway and then see if I could stop in the next 700 feet. Sure enough, I was eventually able to do it. Years later, I was talking to Holger "Jorgy" Jorgensen (one of the most outstanding pilots in Alaska that I flew with), who did a lot of flying in the DC-3 on the North Slope. He said they routinely landed on the 700-foot runways.

At Wien Airlines, we were still doing a lot of DEW Line radar installations flying when I got out of the Air Force. The DEW Line mostly had been completed by then but it required the services of an air service to continue to maintain these installations. There were larger installations situated at intervals, starting from the western part of Alaska's northern coastline extending east across Alaska to the north coast of Canada. In between the larger installations were smaller sites with shorter runways that were usually serviced by smaller airplanes. Sometimes the DC-3 could land at these smaller stations in the hands of pilots like Bob Rice and Holger Jorgensen with bigger loads but this was not a contract requirement.

The weather at Alaska's north coast was usually worse than weather in the Interior. There was a lot of coastal fog. The larger installations like Point Barrow and Barter Island usually had ground-controlled approach capability using radar. The radar final approach controller became very good at telling you what heading and glide path corrections to make in order to put you a few feet above the runway so you could then land visually. The normal minimum weather authorized for landing was a 200-foot ceiling and half-mile visibility but due to the importance of these sites, there seemed to be no minimums, unofficially. We very often landed with a 100-foot ceiling and one-eighth-of-a-mile visibility assisted by fifty-gallon barrels lined up on the approach end to guide the pilot to the runway.

When GCA was not operating, we developed our own procedure with an automatic direction finder approach. At Barter Island, I had a procedure to home in on the beacon on the 270 degree bearing, letting down over the water until we could see waves or floating ice cakes and felt safe to go lower. When I crossed the coastline, I turned left to 060 degrees and the runway was right there. I remember once letting down to about 100 feet over the water and when I asked the co-pilot to lower the gear as we approached the shore, he reached down for the gear and then hesitated. He looked out the window and didn't think there was enough room for the gear between the airplane and the water, but with some reassurance he did as I directed.

ONE OF THE FIRST THINGS I DID AFTER active duty in the Air Force was to buy a Super Cub along with skis and floats. The wolves were devastating the moose population at that time so the US Fish and Wildlife Service put a bounty on the wolves. The Super Cub was a great tool to be able to go out and shoot the wolves from the air and a lot of pilots used their planes to make some extra money with this program. In addition to the bounty, the wolf hides were worth an additional fifty dollars. One pilot bought a brand-new Super Cub and became so good at tracking and shooting that he paid for the airplane in one season. The trick was that after shooting a wolf, you had to find a place to land to pick it up without tearing up the fuselage on the brush.

The usual way to get the wolves was to carry a gunner in the backseat with the hope that he wouldn't shoot the wing struts off but some pilots figured out how to fly alone to do their bounty hunting. Don Sheldon at Talkeetna mounted shotguns on the wing struts of his Super Cub and rigged it so he could fire from the cockpit. Wien pilot George Thiele flew and did the shooting alone by trimming the airplane nose up and holding the nose down with his knees on the stick. As soon as he fired, he just opened his legs, which initiated the climb before he hit the ground.

The bounty hunts could be done only in winter when the ground was covered with snow. The key to success was to be able to track the wolves and determine how many there were in the pack, which way they were traveling, how old the tracks were, and how far ahead the wolves were. I asked a good tracker to fly with me and teach me how to track. I never did get the hang of it but one day I did stumble upon a wolf. My gunner used up a lot of ammunition before finally getting it. Before long, I gave up on this moneymaking venture and the program was eventually discontinued.

The Super Cub is a great plane for Alaska where there are few roads. The airplane fills in for a car and allows transportation to areas otherwise inaccessible for fishing, hunting, camping trips, or just going to a remote cabin. We did a lot of waterskiing on Harding Lake, which is about forty miles southeast of Fairbanks. One day someone got the idea that we should try waterskiing behind my Super Cub. I hope I wasn't the one who came up with that harebrained idea. Since we did not have any kind of a quick release hook, we just tied the towrope in a V arrangement to the rear spreader bar where it attached to each float. We were a little concerned about not being able to quickly release the rope in case anything went wrong, but we figured, "Oh, well." We flipped a coin to see who would be the first to be towed. My brother won so I flew the airplane. As it turned out my brother actually lost the coin toss because it was not a good experience for him.

The plan was to have him start out on the bow of a moving boat, wearing two skis, and have the airplane pull him off the bow when he had enough speed to stay on top of the water, with the hope that he would not fall in the water and get run over by the boat. Once we were all set up, I applied full power and the airplane climbed up on the step. I knew that it would be important to fly at the lowest possible speed. At about 40 mph I yanked the Cub into the air. I was a little slow in reducing power and the Cub accelerated very quickly before I was able to get the airspeed back down to just above flying speed. I should have landed right away to see if Richard survived the higher speed but it felt like he was still on the rope. Apparently, he was leaning forward so much trying to hang on that he knew if he let go he would immediately fall backwards. He was praying that I would set the plane back in the water so he could avoid a nasty spill. Finally his strength gave out and I knew he had let go because the airplane started to pitch down and then up as the wooden handles sank below the water and then were flung out and forward. Our friends in the boats that were following us saw arms and legs cartwheeling along the top of the water. When the splashing subsided, they didn't see Richard. Finally a pair of bloodshot eyes appeared as he gradually came to the surface.

It was now time to reassess the operation. Because there was so much drag using two skis, we decided that as soon as the skier was off the boat he would drop one of the skis. Since Richard had been used up, another expendable victim, Austin Ward, volunteered. The one ski operation turned out to be very successful with half the drag.

I was now getting more proficient at leaving the water and maintaining a very low flying speed. Since I had to fly on the back side of the power curve, large power corrections were necessary. Flight time was limited because the engine would get hot, lacking cooling speed. Eventually I was able to tow two water-skiers at the same time.

When I thought that we had all the bugs worked out, I decided to try it. Richard flew the Cub. Let me tell you, that was a thrilling experience. It felt like I was going 100 mph.

About thirty years later, I saw a television program called *That's Incredible*. It showed an airplane towing a water-skier while the narration said it was the first time this had ever been done. Richard and I wished that someone had taken movies of us.

IN 1957, MY CUB WAS LOST IN A tragic accident. Late one summer night I got a telephone call from a very good friend, Dick Moorhead, who was a DC-3 captain for Wien Airlines. He wanted to know if he could use my Cub on floats to look for his friend and fellow Wien captain, Pat Hendricks, who was overdue from a fishing trip to Beaver Creek with his father. Because it was midsummer, it was light all night long, so Dick left with my plane that night.

Uncle Sig called me early the next morning and asked me if I had lent my Cub to Dick. I said I had. He then told me Dick had been killed in my Cub. What a shock. Dick was a very qualified pilot and I had had no reservations about lending him the Cub.

We later found out the story from Pat: When Dick located Pat on a gravel bar on Beaver Creek, he saw that Pat had a flat tire. Dick flew back to Fairbanks and located a spare tire and wheel and flew back to Pat's location.

He couldn't land near Pat because there was not enough water there so he air-dropped the tire to him. After he made the drop, he circled back to yell something out the open door. He was flying into the early sunrise and did not see a tall tree ahead. The right wing hit the tree and the airplane cartwheeled and hit the ground inverted, exploding on impact. Dick was killed instantly, leaving behind a wife and four children.

In those days, few pilots and airplane owners thought about insurance and I didn't have any insurance on my Cub. Dick's wife told me that I could have their Cub in exchange for the loss of mine. She wanted to pay me for the floats as well, but I declined.

I FLEW THE DC-3 FOR ABOUT 1,200 HOURS before Dick King would let me fly the C-46. Dick was a World War II pilot and a fine man and he carried the airline on his back for many years. He was greatly respected by the pilots and if he said, "Jump," we jumped.

From a distance, the C-46 looks like a larger DC-3 but the handling characteristics are very different. It is an amazing airplane capable of hauling big loads into short fields and onto snow-laden, frozen lakes. It was not as easy to fly as the DC-3, but it handled very nicely once you learned how to fly it. Initially the C-46 was certified only to fly cargo in civilian operations. Eventually it was certified Transport Category after modifications were completed and it became our mainline passenger airplane for years.

While I was in the Air Force, Wien Airlines operated about eight C-46s for the construction of the DEW Line. After I returned to Wien, most of the Dew Line construction was completed but the airplane continued to be in demand since no other airplane could do the job a C-46 could do for the cost. The airplane was also needed by oil and geophysical companies to haul loads to the North Slope to support oil exploration. The C-46 could haul 14,000-pound loads and we could land it on frozen lakes. It would handle fairly deep snow conditions but we had to check out the lake ice thickness ahead of time. If the lake ice was blown clear of snow, the ice was usually very thick. If there was snow on the ice, it acted like a blanket and the ice usually was not as thick. We needed about three feet of ice to be safe. Before we landed a C-46 on lake ice, I flew there in a Cessna 180 to determine the thickness using an ice auger.

The C-46 was a very reliable airplane, but flying most airplanes is never dull. One day on a passenger flight in the C-46 with co-pilot Doug Millard, we were climbing out of Nome after dark, heading for Kotzebue. It was Doug's leg to fly and I was in the right seat. Suddenly the left engine fire warning light came on accompanied by a very loud bell. Quite often we got false fire warning indications so I asked Doug to look out his side to see if there was any sign of a fire. He looked at it for a few seconds as I anxiously waited and finally said, "Yup, it's on fire." I immediately initiated the shut-down checklist and activated the fire bottle. We turned around to return to Nome. The light stayed on but we were able to silence the loud bell. After landing we learned that it actually was a false fire warning. This really puzzled Doug. After thinking about what he saw, he realized that he had seen the reflection from the rotating beacon bouncing off the rubber seal that was between the engine cowling and the nacelle. As the beacon rotated it changed the intensity of the reflection and it looked like flames. But we would have had to shut it down and fired the bottle anyway. Better to be safe than sorry.

Another time I was leaving Nome in the C-46 for Kotzebue with co-pilot Don Hulshizer and a plane full of passengers when the main cargo door, which was hinged at the top and had the passenger door built into it, blew open. Our flight attendant, Eleanor Johnson, was just walking by it with a tray of food for the passengers when a whole lot of sky appeared. Suddenly I realized that a lot of air was flowing through the cockpit and as I turned around to look at the cabin (we did not lock the cockpit doors in those days and very often just kept them open), I saw a lot of daylight there just as Eleanor came to the cockpit. The door hadn't been latched properly when we left Nome, which was my responsibility as captain. When we had leveled off, the increased speed of the plane created enough suction to suck it open.

I asked Don to go back and see what he could do but told him to be very careful. I turned around and started a slow airspeed descent back to Nome. I also put the airplane into a left side slip, which helped bring the door down quite a bit. With the help of a passenger, Don was able to grab a rope that was attached to the bottom of the door and gradually pull the door in by threading the rope through the bottom part of the rear passenger seat. He re-latched the door, properly this time, so we turned back around and continued to Kotzebue.

In June 1958 one of our C-46s, piloted by Captain Jim Freericks, went through the ice at Peters Lake while on a supply mission to support studies for the International Geophysical Year in the Brooks Range. This was an important event for Wien Airlines—losing an airplane is no small matter—and the recovery was a huge effort.

Richard had been sent ahead of the C-46 in a Twin Beech 18 to take a three-man crew, camp gear, and equipment to set up the initial camp and to check the ice at Schrader Lake, which was connected to Peters Lake, with a spit in between. At Schrader Lake, he had drilled the ice and found five feet of nice, clear blue ice, which was plenty of ice to support the C-46. The snow had melted off the surface, which made for ideal landing conditions. An Air Force C-119 landed to drop off a boat and other gear for the project. When the C-119 landed, the weight of the aircraft caused a gusher of water to blow out the hole onto the lake. The pilots did not like that and they hastily unloaded and departed. They never came back with the rest of the loads.

Landing the C-46 on frozen lakes was a common occurrence in those days. I did a lot of it, once even in a Boeing 737. There was a time period where the snow would melt off, but there was still good solid ice to support an aircraft. However, when the ice had "candled," meaning the water on the surface flowed through the ice, then the strength of the ice was compromised. The timing on when one could land safely, after the snow melted, had to be monitored carefully: there was usually about a two-week window.

After Richard drilled the ice, there was a delay of about two weeks before the first C-46 load could be brought in. The crew that Richard left at the lake reported that the conditions had remained the same. In the meantime, however, a warm wind and rain had deteriorated the ice, but the crew did not report it. Additionally, for some reason, the Wien flight crew of the C-46 landed on Peters Lake, which Richard had not checked. The ice on that lake could have been a little more deteriorated.

When they landed the C-46, weighing about 46,000 pounds, on Peters Lake, the landing gear went through the ice, but the wings prevented it from going all the way through. We soon began an epic effort to save the airplane. It had recently gone through a complete overhaul, and was needed badly by the airline. It was also Wien's first C-46 and I think we were all attached to it.

The ice on Peters was rotten and would not support any efforts to lift up the plane. The only solution was to float it to where it could be winched out of the lake and flown off the frozen tundra in the fall. At least that was the plan.

Although the ice was not able to support the C-46, we were able to land some Norseman aircraft to deliver a crew and some lifting bags. With DC-3s and a chartered C-82, we air-dropped 140 empty fifty-gallon fuel drums and more lifting bags on the ice, which the crew kicked over to the C-46. Using the lifting bags, they were able to lift the aircraft up enough to insert many of the drums into the belly compartment; the rest were put under the wings and belly in a raft form to keep the C-46 afloat.

Dick King, the chief pilot, ordered Richard to get a set of big tires for his Super Cub and head back up to Peters Lake to support the salvage operation. Jess Bachner had developed a fiberglass liner to adapt Stinson air wheels to Cub wheels. These eighteen-inch tires were some of the first large tires adapted to the Cub. Richard installed them and headed back to Peters Lake with a load of fuel and supplies. Richard made many trips in the Cub to the lake from Barter Island and Fairbanks. The Cub took a beating from the many landings on the tundra, resulting in a bent prop from a nose up and bent gear from all the rough terrain landings. But he simply did a field repair on the prop and continued to fly with the bent gear.

On his last flight from Barter Island to the lake, Richard was talking to Fairbanks on the HF radio when it got very quiet. The engine had frozen from a broken oil line but he was able to do a dead-stick landing on a 300-foot gravel bar. He said it was the best dead-stick landing he ever made.

When the engine cooled down he found that the prop would now turn, but not as freely as it had. He contacted Barter Island on the radio and asked if someone could air-drop him some oil. In a couple of hours, an Interior Airways Cessna 180 dropped him some quarts of oil but most of the quart cans burst when they hit the gravel bar. He was able to salvage about six quarts. The only thing he could do to stop the oil leak was to run the good oil line from the cooler back into the engine and bypass the cooler. He was able to get the engine running and depart for Peters Lake where there was a mechanic. He landed with the oil temperature extremely hot and would not have been able to go much farther without the oil cooler. After some temporary repairs with parts from the C-46, he flew the Cub to Fairbanks. The Cub needed new landing gear and an engine and prop overhaul.

By this time, the ice had melted and chief pilot Dick King told Richard to go check himself out in the Norseman on floats and get back up to Peters Lake with fuel, tools, parts, and equipment. When he landed at Peters Lake, the crew had towed the C-46 to the north end of the lake where the flat spit area was and had been able to winch the aircraft out of the lake. In addition to helping the crew get the C-46 airworthy, he made about twenty flights to Barter Island for equipment and supplies. His flights to Barter Island usually involved heavy coastal fog extending onshore so he had to learn the landscape very well to navigate for the last few miles in low visibility and then land and taxi in zero-zero conditions to the lagoon near the airport.

When the C-46 was ready to fly, they had to wait until October when the tundra froze enough to support the plane for departure. The C-46 was then flown to Barter Island and then successfully on to Fairbanks. It went on to fly for many more years with Wien.

It just so happens that twenty years before this, Wien Alaska Airlines had had a similar experience. My father had purchased a surplus Ford Tri-Motor from Northwest Airlines in Seattle in 1935, using the proceeds from his just-completed pioneering flight at night over the Canadian Rockies to deliver the photos of the Will Rogers and Wiley Post crash. When he returned home with the Ford and about eight passengers, it was the first commercial passenger flight between Seattle and Fairbanks.

The Ford had terrific performance and became a great airplane for Alaska. It could haul 4,000-pound loads into fields as short as 1,200 feet. At least that is what my dad could do with it. In the mid-1930s, it was the largest passenger- and cargo-carrying airplane to come to Alaska.

Each spring, when the snow had melted in Fairbanks, the routine was to fly airplanes to nearby Harding Lake, where the ice was still good for wheels or skis. At the lake, the mechanics would switch the airplanes from wheels to skis so they could continue to operate in the snow country to the north and west.

The winter of 1937–38 there had been a big earthquake that had cracked the ice at the lake, and in the spring the crack caused the ice to start melting prematurely. As my dad taxied across the lake in the Ford to take off into the wind with a full load of passengers, the ice broke and the plane went in up to the wings. All the passengers deplaned without even getting wet but it looked like the Ford was lost. When Sam White heard about it, he put together a team of mining and heavy equipment experts and with poles, cables, pulleys, and timbers, headed for the lake. They worked night and day while my mother cooked for them. Time was the enemy because the lake was thawing fast. They had to remove and straighten the propellers and the engines and magnetos had to be dried out so they would run. It was a miracle that my dad was able to fly it off the lake in just three days with engines sputtering.

I had been in school staring out the open windows again when the Ford flew by on final to Weeks Field.

8

Alaskan Adventures

In addition to flying the DC-3, I also flew the bush planes as often as I could. I did a lot of glacier flying for Wien and also did jobs such as support for mountain climbers on my own time. One day one of the Wien pilots, George Thiele, asked me if I would be interested in accompanying him in my Super Cub on a polar bear hunt he had lined up for a customer. Polar bear hunters always flew in twos in case one of the airplanes broke down or went through the ice. George was a very experienced guide and was in great demand. I had no experience as a guide and was keen to learn how to hunt polar bears. My brother, Richard, also wanted to learn so he borrowed George's brother's PA-11 Cub. We figured if two airplanes are good to have, three are even better. We headed for Barrow with the three airplanes to meet George's customer, who turned out to be cowboy actor and singer Roy Rogers and a cameraman. Roy flew with George, and I had the cameraman. Richard carried the extra camera equipment. We flew all day for about five days as far north as 150 miles from Point Barrow.

Finding polar bears was not an easy thing that late in the season, even for an experienced tracker like George Thiele. In order to find a polar bear out on the ice, you had to know how to track the bear. As with the wolves, you had to know what the tracks were telling you: how old the tracks were, which way they were going, and how many bears there were. Because it was late in the season, there was no new snow, which was what we needed to find the tracks. The only tracks we could find were old so we weren't having much luck.

On the fifth day, George came down with severe appendicitis during the flight and when we landed back at Barrow, he was rushed to the hospital. That ended our expedition. Having his pilot fall ill scared Roy so much that when he got back to California, he took flying lessons. About a year later I visited him at his ranch and he asked me if there was enough room on the ranch to operate an airplane. "Not quite," I told him.

Richard had already arranged for two of our friends, distinguished Fairbanks businessmen, to come up for a hunt after the hunt with Roy Rogers. We had figured that by then, of course, we would have been experienced bear hunters. Richard called them and told them not to bother coming because it was too late in the season to do any tracking. Plus, the old ice was rough and it would be hard to find a place to land. They said they were coming anyway because they just wanted to get out of town.

We decided we would simply give them a tour of the Arctic ice. But to our surprise, just an hour and twenty minutes out of Barrow, we stumbled on a nice, big bear. My only thought was, *Oh, no. What do we do now?* I had the first hunter in my plane so I started to look for an area that was smooth enough to land on. I had no idea how the bear would react when we landed near him so I picked a spot just within shooting distance in case he turned around and charged before we could get out of the plane and start shooting. But by the time we landed and climbed out of the airplane, the bear was already out of range. He was on a course to the northeast so I decided to fly in that direction, land, and let him come to us. It took some time to finally find ice that was smooth enough to land on. But again, as soon as we touched down, the bear changed course to the northwest and when we got out of the airplane he was out of range.

By this point I had figured out that we could land closer and the bear probably would not charge. The next time I landed right on his tail so as to be close enough to shoot by the time we got out of the airplane. As soon as we had our feet on the ground, my hunter started firing, and missing. I was afraid that the bear was going to be out of range soon so I picked up my gun and shot, putting the bear down. For the record, however, I am sure that my hunter made the fatal shot.

One of the hunters had some experience in skinning elk so we were able to get the job done in about an hour and a half. George could have done it in about twenty minutes.

I knew that it had been incredible luck that with no tracking abilities we had found, and shot, that bear. I didn't think we would find another but we decided to go again the next day. I had the other hunter in my airplane and we had been out only about twenty minutes when we spotted another bear. I could not believe it. Since we were now experienced polar bear hunters, we landed, shot, and skinned the second bear. We hauled back as much meat as we could to give to the Iñupiat Eskimos at Barrow. Our two hunters were very happy and they each ended up with a nice polar bear rug.

In later years when I was doing helicopter flying, I did some work on the side with the US Fish and Wildlife Service to tag polar bears north of Point Barrow to keep track of where they were migrating and to get a count of how many bears there were on the ice pack. The big question was: do they stay close to the coastal areas or are they ranging all over the ice as far as the North Pole? There was by then increasing concern that the polar bear might become an endangered species. Our Hiller 12E4 was flying out of Barrow but after being on the job for a while, our pilot had to leave. We did not have a replacement pilot so I was able to get time off from the airline to take his place. I also thought this might be my chance to finally learn how to track a polar bear. The two fish and wildlife agents I carried were very good at it and so we found quite a few bears. If a bear did not already have a big number spray-painted on its hide, one of the agents fired a tranquilizer into the bear's rear end. To do this, we needed to get as close to the bear as possible for accuracy, but sometimes when we got close, the bear would turn around and try to swipe us out of the air. A good yank on the collective was required. After the agent landed a dart, we circled until the bear laid down.

At first I was hesitant to trust the tranquilizer, so when I landed, I always kept the engine running for a while. Sometimes the tranquilizer did not take so they had to shoot a second one. The agents took the bear's temperature and determined its age by pulling a tooth that it didn't need. Some bears were weighed, which was done by rolling the bear onto a net and hooking the net to a rope tied to the sling hook with a scale attached on the bottom of the helicopter. Tony Oney and Jim Harrower, "Hoppy," from Anchorage, followed us around in two Cessna 180s. They had an Australian onboard who was part of a privately financed program that had designed a radio beacon into a collar for the bears so the bear movements could be tracked. These were attached to the bears after the fish and wildlife team had finished their work. The bears were then numbered with a black spray can so they wouldn't be tagging the same bear again.

I never heard how the census turned out, but it wasn't long before polar bear hunting by air was stopped in the early 1970s.

DURING THE 1957 INTERNATIONAL GEOPHYSICAL YEAR, WIEN AIRLINES got a contract to fly support for a scientific team that was setting up camp on the McCall Glacier in the Brooks Range in northern Alaska.

Even though my father's old friend Joe Crosson had made what was probably the first landing on a glacier, the Muldrow Glacier, in 1932 in a Fairchild 71—a plane that was much larger than the Super Cub—in 1957 it was thought that it would not be feasible to land any airplane bigger than a Super Cub on the glacier. There was a well-known glacier pilot at Talkeetna who had been hauling a lot of climbers in a Super Cub and he, too, believed that the Cub was the largest airplane that you could safely use. The Wien chief bush pilot started the job using his Super Cub and when his vacation time came, chief pilot Dick King asked me to continue the job with my Cub.

After completing the first trip, I told Dick that a Cessna 180 would work just fine there. Dick trusted my judgment and we continued to use the 180 after that. I might have been the first to use a 180 on the Kahiltna Glacier on the south side of Mount McKinley. When the chief bush pilot returned from vacation to continue the McCall flights with his Super Cub, he was upset that I was using the Wien Airlines Cessna 180 but he begrudgingly finished the contract with that plane.

In the early 1960s, the Alaska Air National Guard flew to the Juneau Ice Cap on the Taku Glacier with the Fairchild C-123 on retractable wheel skis, a plane bigger than the DC-3. Now they are using even larger airplanes to haul mountain climbers, like the de Havilland Beaver and the single engine Otter. On the big glaciers, even a DC-3 on skis would work fine.

During this assignment, I found out that there was a lot to learn about glacier flying. The first thing I learned was that there is no natural horizon when you are in among the mountains. When you are on final approach on landing, heading up-glacier, there is a tendency to be too low because the touchdown point very often is above your altitude on final and, lacking the sight picture of the real horizon, it is easy to think the glacier incline is more level. This sometimes requires full throttle in order to climb enough to avoid landing short. I learned that whenever possible, I should try to make a pass down-glacier so I could determine the altitude at my desired landing point. Then I set up my angle to the runway based on altitude, not on how it looked. Using this method, it looked like I was going to overshoot, but I found that the glacier came up fast.

I also learned to check out the side slope on my down-glacier pass. When I made my first landing at the 8,000-foot level on McCall, I noticed at the last minute that the side slope was substantial and because no go-around was possible, I had to go to full power and turn into the slope before touchdown. In the larger airplanes, it was especially important before coming to a stop to go to full power after touchdown and, at just the right speed, to push forward on the wheel and lift the tail out of the snow while doing a 180 degree left turn to end up pointing downhill. If you stopped before making the turn-around, the slope could be so steep that you might not have enough power to do it, especially with non-turbocharged engines at higher altitudes.

With my interest in glacier flying, I noticed an article in *Flying Magazine* about a pilot who had done some landings in the Rocky Mountains near Aspen, Colorado, in a Cessna 180. My friend Austin Ward and I happened to be skiing in Aspen in 1957 so I decided to look up the pilot, whose name was Tommy. He invited me for dinner where we talked about glacier and mountain flying and he invited me to fly with him the next day to the mountains, where we planned to do just a landing and a takeoff. There was a recent layer of snow of about four feet throughout the mountain areas, which was of some concern to me due to the possibility of the airplane getting stuck.

Because of the magazine article, I had assumed Tommy had some mountain flying experience; however, he was not skilled in mountain flying. This first became apparent when we started down the runway at Aspen and he slammed the throttle in and put both hands on the wheel. I had never seen anyone do that before and the thought came to me that I might be in trouble. Once we neared the mountains, he picked out an area at an elevation of about 12,000 feet. I had not landed this high before and I hoped that

ARCTIC INSTITUTE OF NORTH AMERICA

OFFICES: 3485 UNIVERSITY STREET, MONTREAL 2, P Q · 2 EAST 63RD STREET, NEW YORK 21, NEW YORK
1530 P STREET, N W, WASHINGTON 5, D C · 388 ELGIN STREET, OTTAWA 4, ONTARIO

New York Office

August 1st 1957.

Mr. Merrill Wien,
Wien Alaska Airlines,
Box 649,
Fairbanks, Alaska.

Dear Merrill,

Just a note to tell you how much I appreciated all you
did to make our visit to the McCall glacier such a success.
As I think I mentioned to you, I have made several hundred
glacier landings in my life but none which gave me a greater
feeling of personal security and competence of the pilot than
those of last week.

The project is most fortunate in having your interest
and ability at its disposal.

I will be in Alaska again in October and hope that we
will be able to visit the glacier again together.

With warmest regards,

Yours very sincerely,

Walter A. Wood,
Director, AINA, Inc.

WAW:JB

Walter A. Wood, Director of the Arctic Institute of North America, sent this letter after I
had flown him to the McCall Glacier in 1957 in bad weather, landing at the geophysical
camp at 8,000 feet.

he knew what he was doing. We touched down fine but he was too late adding power to get the airplane turned around and pointed downhill. We got about halfway around when the plane came to a stop, sliding sideways. The skis knifed into the snow, leaving the airplane tilted at a very steep angle.

We went to work shoveling the airplane out of the deep snow but we had only our skis, which we happened to have with us, to shovel with. We finally got the airplane level and pointed downslope but while it had been tilted, half of the fuel had drained out through the vent tube. At that point, I should have insisted on doing the takeoff but I think the altitude limited my judgment. Instead, I suggested Tommy take off alone and then land again so I could take movies of it. He put half flaps down and started his takeoff before I could get his attention. With the flaps down, rudder control is reduced because the flaps deflect the air down and away from the rudder, and the torque overpowers any rudder correction. We also had a left crosswind, which compounded the problem with directional control. What he should have done was leave the flaps up on the initial roll until he knew he had good directional control and then pop the flaps. With the flaps down, he was not able to keep the airplane straight and it veered to the left, again knifing into the snow at a steep angle and almost flipping upside down. The left wing was now sticking up, which caused the rest of the gas to drain out. This time the plane was really stuck and it was getting dark.

Tommy may have been a poor mountain pilot but he was a good skier. I was not a good skier, especially in four feet of new snow. Fortunately, my friend Austin and many others were watching through binoculars from a sundeck at the top of a ski run. They saw us leave the airplane and knew that if we skied down, we would end up at the highway, so they headed that direction. It was still light when we left the airplane but it soon got dark. Fortunately, there was a full moon to light the way. I was loaded down with cameras and every time I tried to make a fancy turn to avoid the trees, I instead went straight into the trees and found myself buried upside down in the deep snow. It took a lot of energy to get back up on my skis every time this happened. Tommy had no problem sashaying left and right down the slope.

We thought that the highway was just over the next ridge but when we got to the other side, there was no road. There were actually two more climbs and descents before we came to the road, only to find out that it was closed for the winter. We then had to ski quite a distance on the road until we finally came to the point where it had been plowed. Our friends were there, with thermoses of coffee in hand, to pick us up. I was not a coffee drinker but that coffee sure tasted good. I was totally exhausted.

The word got around Aspen about what had happened. Several people told me that the last time Tommy flew up to the glacier, he had wrecked his airplane and they had to haul it off the mountain in pieces. Apparently, our flight was his first with his new airplane.

I TRADED IN MY SUPER CUB TOWARD THE purchase of a Cessna 180 and I applied for an air taxi certificate, as did Richard with his Super Cub. We wanted to get paid for some of the flying we were doing but we had to have a certificate to do it legally as we continued to fly support for climbers. I hauled some climbers to Mount McKinley, checked on them during their climb, and picked them up when they came off the mountain. And Richard and I did some airdrops to climbers at about 18,000 feet without oxygen. It is one thing to be without oxygen that high but to also be working hard to throw out bundles of supplies was something that almost wiped us out. We learned to take oxygen along on climbing support jobs after that.

Another time, I was using my Beech Bonanza to periodically check on a group of mountain climbers on Mount McKinley. One day on my way to the airport, I stopped at a store to get a roll of film for my camera, only to find the store was closed for the next fifteen minutes. I elected to go without the film because the day was overcast and I did not think that I would have much chance of making it to the mountain that day anyway. I took off and it wasn't long before the overcast ended and there was blue sky as far as I could see to the south. I started my climb and when I reached the mountain at 21,000 feet, lo and behold, I saw the first climber reaching the top. I did have oxygen this time so I was able to circle around the mountain looking down and watching the rest of the group reach the top. The climbers were thrilled because they thought that I was taking pictures of them waving from the highest mountain in North America. . . .

IN EARLY 1958, I WAS CALLED INTO THE chief pilot's office. Dick King said, "I am putting you on a Cessna 180 for a couple of months." My first thought was, *What did I do to deserve that?* I thought that I might have been demoted for some reason because the 180 pay was quite a bit less than the C-46 pay.

Then I found out that I had been requested by Lowell Thomas Sr. to fly for him and I would still get C-46 pay. He was producing a television series called *High Adventure* with his son, Lowell Thomas Jr., featuring locations all around the world and this episode was going to be about Alaska.

Wien Airlines had just taken delivery of a brand-new Cessna 180 and it was given a beautiful Wien paint job. When the time came, I headed for Edmonton with wheel skis mounted on the airplane. There I met Lowell Thomas Jr., his wife, Tay, and their three-year-old daughter Anne, who were going to be flying with us as well. Lowell Jr. was also flying a Cessna 180 that he and Tay had flown to many countries in the Far East. Lowell Sr. was going to join us at locations at Whitehorse and the Juneau Ice Cap to do his narrations. Lowell Jr. had been a B-25 instructor for the Army Air Corps during World War II. I also met the film director, JP, and the cameraman, Mike Murphy, who traveled in my airplane.

The first month we headed for Juneau since they did most of their filming on the Juneau Ice Cap where glaciologist Dr. Maynard Miller had set up camps for glacier studies with his students from the University of Idaho. Lowell Thomas Sr. was including these glacier studies in his show and he had also invited some well-known skiers, including Don and Gretchen Fraser and brothers Pepi and Franz Gable, to the ice cap to be featured in some very unusual skiing. Gretchen had been the first female US gold medalist in Olympic skiing in 1948. Pepi and Franz were German World War II veterans from Austria. Pepi had been an ME109 fighter pilot and Franz had been an infantry soldier on the Eastern front for four years. After the war, they were instrumental in teaching Americans how to ski. They also helped establish ski resorts in Idaho, Washington, and Oregon. Ski photographer John Jay was also invited.

They conducted most of the filming operations from Camp 10 on the edge of the Taku Glacier, at about 6,000 feet in elevation. I noticed that there was a beautiful ski slope behind Camp 10. The skiers wanted to check it out so I made several trips, shuttling them to a nice ridge at the top. When I had them all on top, they headed down the slope. They said it was fantastic skiing so I became the ski lift and made several trips taking them back up to the top with the airplane. This made for some great filming and we had a lot of fun. One time I even towed skiers behind my plane (but not when it was flying).

Much of the filming was done in and around big crevasses with Lowell Sr. talking to Dr. Miller about why glacier studies were so important and what they were learning. Dr. Miller shared how they had learned from core samples what the weather cycles had been in previous years, how fast glaciers were moving, and how the movement was affected by snowfall.

Flying around the top of the ice cap made me imagine what it might be like flying over the moon. It was a dramatic landscape. The average height of the snowfield was about 5,000 feet with small mountain peaks sticking up in various places. It is a beautiful sight from the air. When I flew arriving guests to the glacier, I found a way to give them a real treat, or maybe it was a real scare. In one spot there was a break in the ridges surrounding the ice cap. Just beyond it, the land dropped down vertically several thousand feet to Lynn Canal. I would lower the flaps and reduce airspeed as I approached the gap. When I went through the gap, I pushed over to create zero gravity for a few seconds. It gave my passengers the sensation of falling out of the airplane. Sure glad no one had a heart attack.

When we finished filming in the Juneau area and on the ice cap, I talked Lowell Jr. into filming a spectacular shot of a landing and takeoff in an area on the ice cap with beautiful mountains in the background. Lowell Jr. and I, along with a helper, Bill Boucher, departed Juneau airport and I found a great place to land on top of a smooth, rounded mountaintop. I landed close to the top heading uphill and then stopped right at the top. While we were setting up the camera and discussing the action to be filmed, a thin layer of fog formed below us. Not thinking that it would bother us we continued the setup. All of a sudden the fog rose up and completely engulfed us.

I thought that the fog was just an upslope fog due to a change in wind direction. On foot, I marked out a trail to follow for the takeoff downslope that would miss the crevasses. I thought we would be in the clear as soon as we lifted off the mountain so I wasn't too worried about the location of the surrounding mountains, but I marked the trail in the direction to stay clear of crevasses and where I thought I remembered where the mountains were. But as soon as we started the takeoff, my windshield fogged over and I lost sight of the trail. I then kept the same heading on the directional gyro until liftoff. I did not lift off as fast as I thought we would so I pulled full flap to speed the takeoff into clear air as soon as possible. When we did lift off, we stayed in the fog for a while and when we finally broke into the clear, we were flying right alongside of a mountain.

I was not at all proud of my actions that day. I should have waited for the fog to clear, even if it took days. Again, that reinforced the memory of my father telling me to "always bring the airplane back."

AFTER WE FINISHED OUR WORK IN JUNEAU, THE filming moved to Anchorage. While filming there, Lowell Jr. and I flew our two Cessnas to the mouth of the McNeil River, about a hundred miles southeast of Anchorage. It was the time of year when the salmon were moving back upstream to spawn and the brown bears were gathering there to get in on the feast, catching the fish in their mouths as they jumped the rapids. We used the nearby beach as our landing spot. It worked well at low tide, but when the tide was in, my landing field disappeared. I got to thinking that maybe I could take off and land on the upper part of the beach where the slope was fairly steep. Because the beach had a nice curve, it looked like the centrifugal force landing on the upper part would keep me from sliding sideways. Sure enough, it worked fine. I was able to fly back and forth to Anchorage whether the tide was in or out.

One day, the fish and game officer tending watch there said that he had been expecting a guest to visit but that the floatplane had left his guest in the wrong place quite a way down the coast. He would be stuck there until the floatplane was scheduled to come pick him up a few days later.

I said that I would go and see if there might be some place where I could attempt to land. The agent was skeptical but he went with me to point out the location. When I arrived I could see the agent's friend camped out down in a steep ravine with a makeshift shelter. There was no beach area suitable for a landing. Above the ravine there was a smooth, rounded off ridge that I initially thought would work only for a helicopter, but the more I looked at it the more I thought that maybe I could land there. I made a few passes at it, touching down lower and lower on the side of the ridge and rolling up to where it was level. I made about three or four touch-and-gos and finally decided that it would work. I committed and touched down going on a steep angle up the ridge and stood on the brakes. I managed to stop right at the far edge before falling into the ravine. The poor stranded fellow in the ravine had no idea that I was even considering landing there until he saw the nose of the Cessna 180 sticking over the ridge above. I ended up closer to the edge than I anticipated because the brakes faded quite rapidly. He was one happy guy to get out of there because he did not have enough food for a long stay. The takeoff was easier because I simply dropped off over the edge toward the ocean, which was perpendicular to the way I landed.

Many years later Lowell Jr. told me the reason I was requested to fly support for the *High Adventure* project. Lowell Sr. had asked famous Arctic pilot Bernt Balchen for a recommendation, and Bernt gave him my name. He had flown Admiral Byrd across the South Pole as well as many other pioneering flights. Bernt was a good friend of my father's and I was privileged to know him. I was very honored that he had recommended me.

AFTER THE *HIGH ADVENTURE* PROJECT HAD ENDED, I got a call from Lowell Thomas Sr. asking if I could fly him and his wife and another couple, John and Gladys, on a tour of Alaska. They did not want to travel on the regular Wien tourist flights. The only airplane that would be able to handle the four of them with baggage at a reasonable cost was the Twin Beech. The Cessna 180 was too small and the C-46 or the Fairchild F-27 would have been overkill.

I had not flown the Twin Beech before. Richard had many hours in them but he was an unknown to Lowell. So when the time came, Al Mosley, who was chief bush pilot at the time, qualified me with three landings and takeoffs. I was to pick up the Thomases and their friends at Gustavus near Juneau. On the way there, I began to feel sudden changes in the synchronization of the engines. The synchronization would suddenly surge and then go back to a normal sound for a while before it happened again. I was new in this airplane, so this was a big concern.

I finally convinced myself that I was flying behind two of the most reliable engines ever built, so I quit worrying. I landed for my planned stop at Whitehorse, refueled, and then picked up my passengers at Gustavus before returning to Whitehorse for the night.

After a good look at the historic sights of the gold rush days, we departed Whitehorse for Dawson, Yukon Territory, another historic location from the same period. I had John in the front right seat and Lowell, Fran, and Gladys in the cabin. About ten minutes after takeoff from Whitehorse, the right engine quit, just as if I had turned the ignition switch off. This Twin

Beech did not have the full feathering propellers so the propeller continued to windmill. The ability to feather would have reduced the drag substantially but on the plus side, my passengers did not know we had lost an engine.

I scanned the instruments and found no change in fuel pressure and oil pressure. I asked John in the right seat if he could see anything unusual on the right engine. He said everything looked good to him but when I looked back through the windows in the cabin, I saw a solid stream of smoke flowing from under the trailing edge of the wing. Now let me tell you, when you think that your airplane might be on fire, that qualifies as a moment of stark terror.

If there was ever a time when I really wanted everything to go smoothly, this was it. Lowell Sr. had a lot of confidence in me and I did not want anything to happen that would change that.

I couldn't help but be reminded of the saying, "Flying is hours and hours of boredom interrupted by moments of stark terror." After noticing the smoke, I heard Fran say to her friend, "Gladys, do you smell smoke?" I was so glad that she did not look out the right window behind the wing. While doing my best to keep any panic under control, I started a gradual turn back to Whitehorse. If I had been alone I probably would have been more aggressive in my flying but I did not want to show any alarm. I had not yet called the tower but during the turn, when they saw the smoke trail, they called and said, "The fire trucks are on the way."

I shut the fuel off and started to reach for the T-handle under the right seat to discharge the fire bottle, but then I decided to wait until I had more evidence of a fire. The fire warning light had not illuminated yet.

I kept climb power on the good engine and that was enough to get us back to the airport with a gradual descent. When we were rolling out on the landing, the right prop froze to a stop with a screech. That was the first time that my passengers in the back realized that anything was wrong; in fact, they thought we had landed at Dawson.

We spent the night at Whitehorse again and the next day during Lowell's daily national broadcast from Whitehorse, he described our episode and said it was over the location of the "Cremation of Sam McGee" on "the marge of Lake Lebarge," as written by poet Robert Service. He then added something about how that might have also been the location of the cremation of Lowell Thomas.

When the engine on the Twin Beech was overhauled, we found out that some gears had failed, which prevented the sump pump from sending crankcase oil back to the oil tank. This caused the whole power section to fill up with oil, which went past all the piston rings and drowned out all the spark plugs. The oil then continued out the hot exhaust and made all that smoke.

The next day we caught the Wien Alaska Airlines scheduled F-27 flight to Fairbanks. We continued flying around the state on the F-27 scheduled flights and I arranged to be the captain on all the flights they were on.

Lowell Sr. and Jr. were some of the finest people that I have ever met and I count my experiences with them among some of the most memorable of my life. Their character was unquestionable and my association with them was truly inspirational.

Lowell Jr. was no stranger to Alaska when the *High Adventure* project began, but I think he especially enjoyed the glacier and mountain flying. Not too long after we finished filming, he and Tay moved from their home in New Jersey to Anchorage. Lowell bought wheel skis for his Cessna and continued to do glacier flying, as well as making documentaries and writing; he also eventually served as lieutenant governor of the state. After Don Sheldon, founder of Talkeetna Air Service, died, Lowell Jr. bought the company and became well known for his many rescues off Mount McKinley, some as high as 14,200 feet. To my knowledge, he never even scratched an airplane.

9

Branching Out

Alaska had always been plagued with forest fires in the summer, which made visual flight difficult and destroyed a lot of virgin timber. The Bureau of Land Management (BLM) was responsible for fighting the fires and they had four B-25s on contract, which could each haul about a thousand gallons of borate to drop on fires as soon as they were reported. Having been trained in the B-25 during my time in the Air Force, I saw a possible business opportunity there. In 1959, Richard and I asked the BLM if they would put another B-25 on contract. They said they had enough for the time being but that they would let us know if they needed another one.

We gambled anyway and submitted a bid on a B-25 to the War Assets Administration at Davis-Monthan, in Tucson, Arizona. We successfully bid $2,750 on a low time B-25 with only 240 hours since IRAN (inspection and repair as necessary). I could not get the time off to go pick up the plane so my friend Jim Coin, a Pan Am Stratocruiser captain, volunteered to pick it up from Ryan Field near Tucson. He flew it to Idaho where we had a 1,000-gallon tank installed. Then Richard and Jim flew it to Fairbanks. When the airplane arrived in Fairbanks, we had to do a very thorough inspection before we could get it licensed with the FAA. During the inspection we discovered that all the fabric on the control surfaces needed to be replaced. By the time we had it ready to go in late summer, the fire season was over. As the summer of 1960 rolled around, BLM put us on contract for $400 an hour. We hired a Wien pilot on leave from Wien Airlines, Harold Pilcher, for that summer's flying. It was a fairly good fire season that year and we managed to do quite well financially. Harold and Richard had one ten-hour day making drops out west near Haycock and so we paid for the airplane with just that one day. I was married by this time and my wife, Kathy, and I had our first child—Kim, born the previous winter.

The second summer we hired Rudy Billberg as pilot of the B-25. Rudy was a very experienced pilot with a great reputation. When I checked him out in the plane, I thought he might be dropping the load a little too high so I demonstrated how I thought it should be done. I made my pass along the fire line and flew into heavy smoke. When we came out of the smoke, there was a lone, very tall tree in front of us. I just missed it with a sharp, climbing left turn. When we got back on the ground Rudy said, "Merrill, we have to talk."

I said, "Rudy, I was wrong. You do it the way you want to do it." After that, Richard and I—and BLM—were very happy with his flying.

WE FELT THAT WE HAD DONE SO WELL the first year, we decided to buy another B-25 that was available in Fairbanks from Al Mosley. During the summer of 1960, we were also talked into buying a helicopter from the Hiller factory. BLM was using helicopters to recover the first fire fighters that were parachuted onto the fires until another team could be airlifted in.

The Hiller helicopter company had hired a pilot, Link Luckett, to fly a Hiller 12E to Fairbanks from Anchorage to generate some interest in it. I took my first ride ever in a helicopter with Link and I was thrilled with the experience. That was when I told my brother that we had to get into the helicopter business. I guess Link relayed our enthusiasm back to the Hiller factory and it was not long before a Hiller test pilot showed up with a reconditioned Hiller 12E that he intended to leave in Alaska. Richard and I were not ready to take that big step yet but Hiller made us an offer that we couldn't refuse: no payments until the next summer and the Hiller test pilots would train one of us for a commercial helicopter rating. We bought the helicopter and incorporated as Merric, Inc. (from the first three letters of Merrill and Richard). Our very good friends Doug Millard, a Wien pilot, and Stan Halverson, a Wien mechanic, invested in the company as well. Stan took on our maintenance program and Doug took on the secretarial work. We anticipated a very profitable season with two B-25s and a helicopter.

We stored the helicopter in my garage for the winter and I took a vacation from the airline to go to Palo Alto, California, with Stan for the training at the factory. I found helicopters to be more difficult to learn to fly because when you make a correction on any one of the controls, a correction is also needed on the other controls simultaneously. I was beginning to wonder if I would ever be able to learn to fly a helicopter. I think that I had about eight hours of dual instruction when things started to come together. It just took some time before I became a part of the helicopter and the movements became natural, without me having to think about it. By the time I had the required twenty-five hours, I really felt good in the helicopter.

At the end of the thirty days, I took my check ride with the FAA and I was anxious to show the examiner my proficiency with auto rotations. My examiner said, "Oh, no. We won't be doing any auto rotations." And he proceeded to do most of the flying. In those days helicopter pilots were few and far between and although the inspector was helicopter rated, he likely did not feel comfortable handling any screwups I might make. He knew I was trained by the Hiller test pilots and that they would not put me up for the flight test if I wasn't ready for it. So after seeing that I could handle the helicopter quite well, he took the opportunity to get a little more experience himself.

I did not know how good the training I received at Hiller was until we tried to find insurable helicopter pilots. I had only twenty-five hours and the insurance companies did not want to insure me. We hired a 750-hour pilot who was insurable but he was a poor pilot. I had to fly with him to keep him from wrecking the helicopter. That really cut down the payload. We hired another 800-hour pilot and he couldn't fly either. We ended up with a couple damaged helicopters before we were finally able to convince the insurance company to insure me. Because of the flight time restrictions mandated by the FAA for airline flying, I was limited in the time I could fly for Merric so this in turn limited the amount of work the company could take on. Richard and I soon began to wonder what we had gotten ourselves into.

We were hoping to get work with the helicopter hauling smoke jumpers and equipment to fight forest fires but that following summer had the fewest number of fires that the Interior of Alaska had seen for many years.

We sold the two B-25s and also sold the 12E to Livingston Helicopters in Juneau. We then bought an early Hiller 12B from Joe Soloy, a Ketchikan operator. The Hiller 12B was similar but had a smaller engine and was a third of the price of the later 12E version. Joe Soloy lent us some floats for the flight to Juneau, which also gave me an opportunity to practice auto rotations on floats. In Juneau, Livingston Helicopters helped us change to skids and we shipped the floats back to Ketchikan. Stan and I flew the helicopter to Fairbanks.

Our difficulties continued. We had a hard time keeping the spark plugs from fouling in the Hiller 12B's Franklin engine due to the high lead content in the required 91 octane fuel. When one cylinder cut out from fouling, the helicopter would lose so much power that we had to land and change the bad plugs. We eventually came up with a 50/50 mixture of 80 octane and 100 octane, which worked out a lot better until 100 low lead fuel became available.

One day, I was on a charter to the Minto flats area, west of Fairbanks, with two passengers from BLM who were checking on cabin improvements to qualify for land acquisition. I spent a good deal of the time hovering at high power in areas where I could not land and even over rivers and lakes where an engine failure would have been disastrous. After finishing the tasks, we were on our way home when I noticed that the airspeed indicator was showing only about 40 mph. I was flying over a lake that was covered with a lot of rotten ice and was not safe to land on. My first thought was that I might have taken some water into the static port on the helicopter's belly when I was hovering in the water to let my passengers out to wade to shore. This might have caused an erroneous airspeed reading. But I thought I had better detour toward the closest shore in case I lost power. Sure enough, I hadn't quite reached the shore when the engine started a continual backfire and there was not enough power to stay airborne. I stretched the semi-powered glide as far as I could but was not going to be able to make it to shore. There was about ten feet of open water between the ice and the shore, so I instinctively let the helicopter hit the ice so the bounce, along with pulling the collective, would propel me in a slam dunk to the shore. I landed at the edge of the water and shut down. When I got out of the helicopter I fell up to my waist in a hole of water. I had picked the only level place to perch in that area.

I identified the cylinder and the plug that was not firing but the plug would not budge. When we became overdue, Richard asked a Wien C-46 that was airborne on a local training flight to look for us. They flew right over the top of us a couple of times but did not see us so we started walking back to the village of Minto. The walking was very difficult with marshy areas and deep water. We made it in about three hours and when we came out of the trees at the Minto airport, Richard was there with the Bonanza. The first thing he asked was, "What is the condition of the helicopter?" I started to explain the details of the engine problem but he interrupted me: "WHAT IS THE CONDITION OF THE HELICOPTER?!!"

We flew back to Fairbanks and a day later Richard and Stan borrowed a Cub on floats and found enough water to land a mile or so from the helicopter. I had to take a Wien flight so I was not able to help. After a difficult walk they went to work on the helicopter. Stan was able to remove the spark plug and found it clobbered with what they thought were lead deposits. After they replaced it, Richard started the engine and it ran fine with the new plug. Thinking that they had fixed the problem, Richard told Stan, "You walk back to the Cub and taxi it as close to Minto as you can. I'll fly this to Minto and then I'll walk to the Cub from there."

Stan told him, "I'm not going to make that walk again. If you are going, I'm going with you."

The only problem was that Richard was not a helicopter pilot. I had given him only a few hours of unofficial dual instruction in the helicopter. He certainly did not want to take a passenger but Stan made it clear that Richard wasn't going without him.

They made it to Minto and then walked to the Cub and returned to Fairbanks. Richard flew a subcontractor pilot, Quay Jorgensen, to pick up the 12B at Minto. Quay got about as far as I had when he was forced down. Richard saw him go down and was making plans to retrieve the helicopter again when Quay showed up at Minto in the helicopter. Quay had figured out that the engine would run for a while after it cooled off so he made it back to Minto by landing a couple of times and waiting half an hour before he made another short hop. When we got Stan to Minto, he found that because I had to pull a lot of power while hovering in places where I could not land, the high cylinder head temperatures caused one of the pistons to burn. Massive amounts of the piston aluminum deposited on the spark plug, causing detonation and backfiring. We finally got the helicopter back to Fairbanks by changing the piston.

As Richard recalled, he thought that the engine was starting to get rough when he landed at Minto with Stan the first time. Another minute of two would have put him down also.

QUAY JORGENSEN HAD COME TO MERRIC AT A pivotal time for us. Richard had been doing a lot of flying with fixed wing aircraft out of Bettles for the Bear Creek Mining Company, which was a subsidiary of Kennecott Copper Company. They were doing exploration in the Kobuk area and Richard was able to negotiate a helicopter contract with them for the summer. To satisfy the contract, we subcontracted with Quay, an experienced pilot who had his own Hiller 12A model. While he was flying for Bear Creek Mining he experienced an engine failure caused by fouled spark plugs. In the forced landing he damaged the tail boom of the helicopter. Fortunately, we had the B model in reserve in town and were able fly it to him to continue the contract. It did not perform as well as the A model, so he was anxious to get his back on the job.

We got another tail boom and we were able to get it to the town of Hughes, which was about seventy-five miles from where Quay's helicopter was based. Our problem was how to get a twenty-foot boom from Hughes to Kobuk. Our solution was to talk our old friend, the famous Sam White, who was based in Hughes, into strapping it onto his float-equipped Stinson L-5. He had a very harrowing flight, but he got it there. It seems we had so many challenges in our early days with helicopters, but somehow managed to deal with them.

BY 1964, WE HAD SOLD OUR TWO B-25S and had expanded our helicopter business with the addition of five Hiller 12E4s. As our business expanded, it became very difficult for me, Richard, and Stan to devote enough time to Merric because we all had full-time jobs at Wien. We hired Joe Soloy from Ketchikan to be our general manager and we were at last able to hire some great pilots, especially retired Army instructors who were returning from Vietnam.

Joe did not want to spend winters in Alaska so when we shut down for the season, he trucked the helicopters to The Dalles, Oregon, for winter overhaul. In time, due to increased activity on the North Slope and thus increased demand for our services, we found it prudent to operate year-round and so we built a hangar.

About this time the Allison turbine-powered helicopters were becoming available. As oil exploration on the North Slope increased, we invested in the more expensive helicopters that generally were more reliable and more productive. We did have some teething problems but because the turbine engines had fewer moving parts, they were better suited to cold weather operation.

Winter operations were a real challenge on the North Slope and forced us to be innovative. We were plagued with whiteout conditions, flying over landscapes that had very little vegetation showing in the snow. We found that by installing a row of motorcycle lights on the helicopter, nighttime was the best time to fly. Even with the Allison engines, in the extreme cold, the fuel control regulator could freeze up and cause a hot start, requiring a hot section teardown to inspect for damage. This was difficult to do in the middle of nowhere with limited daylight.

The introduction of the turbine-powered engine in helicopters revolutionized the helicopter industry just as the jet engine did with airlines. The jet engines were lighter and more reliable, allowed more hours between overhaul, and were better suited for cold weather operation.

WHEN WE WERE STILL OPERATING THE HILLER 12B with the smaller, piston-powered engine, I did a lot of power line survey flying for Golden Valley Electric between Fairbanks and Big Delta. This required hovering over the power lines trying to use the downwash from the helicopter blades to knock off the snow so the lines would not touch the trees. But sometimes after a thaw and then freeze, the snow turned to ice, which called for other measures. Golden Valley Electric came up with the idea of bringing along a telescoping pole that would extend down when pointed over the side of the helicopter. When we first tried this system, the pole handler laid the telescoping pole on the collective handle on the left side to use as leverage. Not fully understanding how a helicopter works, he did not realize that the down pressure on the collective changed the blade angle, causing the helicopter to drop lower. I had to pull up on the collective with all my strength while screaming for him to stop. We eventually worked out a better system.

We also did a lot of snow survey flying up the Chena River to the head-waters to determine what the runoff would be in the spring. One year, after the snow melted, I took two men to reinforce the poles that marked the depth of snow with bags of cement. I refueled on a gravel bar near the head-waters of the Chena. As I was taking off with a big load of cement bags and water to mix the cement, and just before reaching transitional lift, the big bearing in the tail rotor gearbox slid out and caused the tail rotor pitch to feather in the neutral position. The result was the same as losing the tail rotor altogether. As the helicopter started spinning around, my first reaction was to chop the power. I immediately realized that this was not going to work so I slammed the power back on, but by then the rotor rpm had deteriorated beyond recovery. As I was spinning around, I tried to stop the forward motion as much as possible to get back over the gravel bar and I kept pulling up on the collective to soften the touchdown. I made it back to the gravel bar; the only damage to the helicopter was that I knocked off the pogo stick on the rear boom that protects the tail rotor.

Now we were stranded. Fortunately, that helicopter had an HF radio onboard that used a whip antenna. I could not raise anyone because the antenna was mounted on the belly and was too close to the gravel bar so I took it off and mounted it on top of a tripod made from three dead tree trunks. I was carrying a role of bailing wire to be used at the survey site so I rolled out a length to connect from the terminal on the belly to the antenna on top of the poles. I laid the wire on top of tree branches to keep it from grounding out on the gravel bar. I then retuned the loading coils under the seat to maximize the output signal. Richard, who was not too far away on a trip to Eagle in a Wien Pilatus Porter, heard my first call. The signal was so strong that it was heard far and wide. When Richard returned from Eagle, he flew the Beechcraft Bonanza airplane to nearby Van Curlers Bar to pick up me and my passengers. Later, Richard, Stan, and I flew back up in the Bell G-2 with a spare tail rotor gearbox and we flew both helicopters back to Fairbanks.

In the spring of 1967, Joe had taken a geological group up to the head-waters of the Salcha River. The weather had been low and raining for weeks and Joe was desperate as he was overdue to get them out. He was concerned they were running out of food. Richard, who had recently acquired his commercial helicopter license, and I decided to try to see if we could get to them. We worked our way up the river and landed below a bluff where we thought they were camped. It was foggy and raining hard and we could not see well enough to get to them. We decided to keep the engines running and wait to see if the weather would lift. After awhile it lifted enough to allow us to hover up the hill and land where the geologists were camped. We told them to break camp and load up. In the meantime, the weather came down again and we were engulfed in fog; however, we kept the engine running until the fog lifted again and we made it out.

On the way back Richard said to me on the radio, "Merrill, there is a massive amount of water coming down the river and the creeks." The water was over the banks and covered the valley from one side to the other. The local news in Fairbanks was reporting that the water level would crest at midnight. Richard made some calls to inform the forecasters that there was a lot more water coming down and the river would not be cresting soon. The forecasters did not heed Richard's warning so the people in Fairbanks weren't prepared for what turned out to be the worst flood the city had ever had. Fortunately, Richard and I had recently finished building our new houses up on the hill north of Farmers Loop Road overlooking Fairbanks so we were high and dry. But our old houses were flooded about halfway up the walls.

Not long after we returned to Fairbanks, we went to work with our two helicopters and flew from dawn to dark rescuing people from their roofs and delivering food and water. Richard, Joe Soloy, and I kept the two helicopters flying all day for about ten days. We didn't know if we were going to be paid for our flying, but we had no choice but to keep flying and rescuing. We eventually were paid by civil defense. If we hadn't, it would have been a major economic setback for us.

At one point, I was on my way to the Fort Wainwright hospital in my Hiller 12E4 when I saw Richard land the Bell G-2 at the powerhouse by the Chena River. He had landed in a tight spot with a big fence around the area. I was concerned about him getting out of an area surrounded by a high fence because he was still a fairly new helicopter pilot so on my way back, carrying a bandaged patient, I checked to see if he was still there. The helicopter was gone but there were cushions and debris floating in the river, and a riverboat was trying to pick people out of the water. My first thought was that Richard had gone down in the river. I was relieved to find it was not him but an airboat that had swamped. As I circled, I saw a woman hanging on to a big plastic bag full of clothes, which was barely keeping her head above water. I brought the helicopter near her and was trying to figure out if I could somehow snatch her from the water when the patient in the back yelled out, "Can I help?" Before I could brief him, he scrambled out the door onto the cargo rack to try to grab her. My big concern was whether I could prevent the helicopter from tipping over with all that weight on one side. I lowered into the water as far as I dared, hoping the tail rotor would not touch the water. All of a sudden the helicopter gave a quick lurch as he pulled the woman onto the rack, and, thank heavens, I was able to keep it under control as we lifted out of the water. I did not have much more cyclic left or room before I would run into the trees as we hovered down the river with the current.

Later, when I had a chance to talk to the rescue boat driver, he told me that before I had arrived he was just about swamped and could not have taken one more survivor onboard.

Richard and I continued to help as many people as possible. We were neighbors on the hill and we both hauled many friends up to our houses from their flooded homes. We were without power and water, but I think we each had about fifty guests so we had to try to keep everyone supplied as best we could. Richard had a 300-gallon water tank on his pickup, so after flying all day Richard and I took turns hauling water from a nearby well. One of our neighbors on the hill owned a grocery store. Every morning I picked him up and took him down to his store where I landed on the roof. When I picked him up at the end of the day he usually had a load of groceries for us and our guests.

I knew where most of the Wien employees lived so I paid special attention to those locations. At one point, I saw one of our pilots waving to me so I landed on their roof. They needed food so I lifted off with a list. When I came back they told me that they had had a fire going in the fireplace for heat. The whole family had come outside to watch when I landed the first time. After I left to get the groceries, they went back inside and saw that the downwash from the helicopter had gone down the chimney and had blown open the fireplace doors, spewing hot coals all over the carpet, which then had to be replaced. So much for being helpful!

Joe Cross, one of the Wien pilots who was staying at our house, said he had a freezer full of meat if we could get to it. I dropped him onto the top of his garage and left to rescue more people. I flew by from time to time and saw him pushing the floating freezer out of the house. Later I saw him throw packages of meat up to the garage roof, one at a time. When I saw that he was ready for pickup, I landed. I was flying the Bell G-2 this time and the meat weighed a lot. It looked like I had a straightaway path over a vacant lot and between the houses that would allow me to gain enough speed to start climbing. I lifted off and dropped down to gain speed for transitional lift. Then I hit a telephone wire. I thought it was going to put me down but it snapped just in time.

It was a very long ten days but I'm glad that Richard, Joe, and I were in a position to put our skills and our helicopters to good use. While we paid special attention to helping our fellow Wien employees, we also managed to give support to many other people in the Fairbanks community. I was very fortunate in that the only flood damage I had was to my Bonanza, which required quite a bit of work before it was flyable again. I had seen the water getting close to the Bonanza but I didn't want to take the time to move it to higher ground.

OUR HELICOPTER OPERATIONS CONTINUED TO EXPAND. BY THIS time, Wien Airlines had merged with Northern Consolidated Airlines and the merged seniority list had moved Richard from captain back to co-pilot. It was also at this point, in the spring of 1969, that our general manager, Joe Soloy, decided to leave Merric. Joe was one of the few great helicopter pilots of the aircraft's early years. We came to a friendly separation with him and we found some investors to buy his stock. Part of the separation deal was that Joe could take with him the engineering data that we had completed up to that time on the conversion of Hillers and Bell 47s to turbine power. Joe went on to create a very successful business doing this and I ended up working for him after I retired from the airline.

Merric was now without a full-time manager so Richard decided to leave the airline and take over the management. He proved to be a highly capable manager and his talent became widely known throughout the business community. This was a boom time in Alaska and many aviation companies expanded too rapidly. Then came the bust when the Native American land claims and resulting land freeze shut down oil exploration. Several companies went bankrupt because they had great short-term contracts but had long-term debts. Richard saw this danger and we did not expand beyond our sure income potential, which caught the attention of the National Bank of Alaska. The bank had a small business investment program and they were looking for investments in companies that had demonstrated good management. They told us there were three things that they looked for in a company: management, management, and management. We gratefully accepted their offer to invest in Merric.

In 1972, the Rowan Drilling Company in Texas offered to buy Merric. They already owned Era Helicopters in Anchorage because they saw the future for oil development in Alaska. Merric and Era operated as separate entities for a few years and eventually Merric was merged into Era.

I think Richard was born with a natural business aptitude and we were lucky to have him at the helm during those economically turbulent years. He guided Merric to become a very successful company so in the end this venture of ours was well worth all the difficulties and headaches of the early years.

This picture was taken on the Juneau Ice Cap in 1958 during the filming of the Lowell Thomas *High Adventure* episode about Alaska. From left to right, Hanz Gable, Pepi Gable, Gretchen Fraser, Lowell Thomas Sr., Don Fraser, and Lowell Thomas Jr. The show's director and cameraman are standing in front of the plane.

On the Juneau Ice Cap in 1958 flying for the *High Adventure* series with Lowell Thomas Sr. I am standing next to Lowell Thomas Jr. (right) on top of a mountain above the fog with Devil's Paw shown in the background. Shortly after this photo was taken, the fog rose up and we had to take off in solid fog.

In the early 1970s while flying Merric Cessna 185 on another flight to the McCall Glacier, in the Brooks Range at about 7,000 feet in elevation.

At Galena, Alaska, waiting for weather to improve before proceeding to Nome. From left to right, me, my father, Noel Wien; my mother, Ada Wien; Mrs. Lowell Thomas Sr.; Lowell Thomas Sr.; and friends of the Thomases accompanying them on a tour of Alaska.

During a stop while polar bear hunting, Roy Rogers kneels next to a memorial for Will Rogers and Wiley Post (about thirteen miles southwest of Barrow, Alaska).

Richard and I on the Kahiltna Glacier, 1960.

Stranded on a mountain in Aspen, Colorado. This is the first landing when we lost all the fuel in the right wing. We dug out the plane only to bury it again on a takeoff attempt, losing the rest of the fuel out of the left tank.

This is what happened when Tommy tried to take off after digging out the plane the first time.

Above: Changing a helicopter engine on the job.

Left: Legendary pilot Joe Soloy on a job at McCarthy, Alaska, supporting mining exploration. Joe was the manager for Merric in the beginning.

I had just arrived in Fairbanks, Alaska, from Kenmore, Washington, with this Beaver for Merric operations.

My brother, Richard, at far left standing next to the plane, about to depart for the McCall Glacier. Stan Halverson, Merric partner and director of maintenance, is standing on the wing strut. Don Schieck, Merric accountant, is at the far right.

Airfield debris resulting from the Columbus Day Storm of 1962, Vancouver, Washington. The nose of my Bonanza is on the right.

Left: The Wien DC-4 on Ice Island T-3, 600 miles north of Point Barrow, 1963, during one of the nicer days.

Above: The piston-powered Pilatus and de Havilland Beaver were the first planes available that performed well in the bush, although the Pilatus did not develop its full potential until the piston engine was replaced with a turbine engine.

A de Havilland Twin Otter. *Photo © by Myron Wright.*

In 1958 while filming brown bear catching fish at the mouth of the McNeil River, I was asked to check on a visitor who was dropped off at the wrong place. He was stranded in a ravine and could not move. After making several passes on a dome nearby, I managed to land. The pictures above and below show where I stopped and also the view from the ravine below where the stranded person was located.

10

A New Bush Plane

Most of the airplanes that were built from the late 1920s through the 1930s could be called bush airplanes; in the early years of aviation in the United States, you might say aviation in the whole country was a bush operation.

Some great bush planes were built during that time, such as the high wing Bellancas, Stinsons, Travel Airs, and Cessna Airmasters. My dad purchased five Airmasters before World War II because it was a very efficient airplane and met the need for smaller loads. With a 145 hp Warner engine, it had a cruising speed of about 145 mph. After World War II, Cessna came out with the Cessna 170 with a 145 hp Continental engine and it cruised only about 120 mph. The Cessna 170 was easier to fly, had better forward visibility from the cockpit, and had more modern construction, but the Airmaster was more efficient. Later models of the Airmaster came out with a 165 hp engine with an even faster cruise speed.

After World War II, the only airplanes being built were airplanes more suited to larger, paved airports. Before the war, my dad and Uncle Sig tried to convince Cessna to put a high lift flap on the Airmaster but as bigger runways were being built throughout the United States, Cessna thought that it was more important to have a flap that would slow the airplane for landing only and not lower landing speed. They did not want the pilot to have to deal with trim changes when flaps were lowered. They did not see a big market in the Alaska and Canadian bush and so Wien Airlines instead bought Army surplused Noorduyn UC-64s, which were well-suited to bush flying. Actually, the best flap that the Airmaster had was their first production model, the C-34, which was built in 1934 and had a trailing edge flap. This gave the airplane the best short field capability of all the Airmasters built. In 1948, when Cessna starting building an all-metal version of the Airmaster, the 5-place Cessna 195, it also had a mid-wing flap. If the 195 had been designed with a trailing edge, Fowler-type flap, the market for it would have been much greater in Alaska and Canada.

Cessna missed an opportunity to fulfill a large need for high-performance bush planes immediately after the war—a big market that was captured instead in 1948 by the de Havilland Beaver and Otter and later in 1959 by the Pilatus Porter, which were the first modern bush planes. When Cessna came out with the 4-place 170 in 1948, it had a small flap. In 1953, they changed to a high lift Fowler-type flap. The same year, the Cessna 180 with 225 hp came out with the same improved Fowler flap as the 170. The added horsepower made the 180 a big hit in Alaska and Canada but we also needed a larger high-performance, short field airplane.

Uncle Sig became interested in the piston engine Pilatus Porter, built in Switzerland. In 1961, Wien purchased one Pilatus Porter with a piston-powered, GSIO 480 Lycoming engine of 340 hp, which was shipped to Fairbanks in a crate. The airplane turned out to be well designed but was underpowered. Later, the Pilatus company installed the French built Turbomeca Astazou turboprop engine. We purchased one and Richard picked it up after it was shipped to the East Coast from Switzerland. This was the first single engine turboprop airplane to be certified in the United States.

Uncle Sig thought that Fairchild might be interested in building the Porter so after getting permission from the Pilatus factory in Stans, Switzerland, he told Richard to stop at the Fairchild factory in Hagerstown, Maryland. With Pilatus test pilot Rolf Böhm, Richard flew the airplane to the Fairchild factory. As it turned out, Fairchild was interested in producing an airplane that might qualify for the upcoming counterinsurgency mission (COIN) for the anticipated military requirement. The Fairchild staff climbed all over the airplane and took many pictures. Pilatus granted authorization to Fairchild to build the Porters under license and they sold many planes to the military. Wien Airlines eventually bought five more from Fairchild with the Pratt and Whitney PT-6 engines and operated them successfully for many years. Later, as better landing areas were built for the growing need, the Twin Otter and Shorts Skyvan became available.

When our turboprop Porter arrived in Fairbanks, I remember a mechanic saying when the cowling was lifted, "I see the heater, but where is the engine?" Wien Airlines eventually bought three of the Astazou Porters, which had outstanding performance with twice the horsepower and a lighter weight engine. However, they were plagued with engine problems. The Turbomeca Astazou was basically a good engine but it had just one battery so in cold weather, hot starts were a big problem.

Because it was a newly developed engine, the PT-6 caused us some teething problems. When Richard arrived with the first PT-6 Porter, I jumped in and made a local flight. I landed at Metro Field, a nearby airport, and when I shifted out of the beta high rpm position after landing, the engine flamed out. The next day Richard took the Porter to Eagle with a load of schoolkids returning for the summer. As he set up for landing, he shifted the engine to the beta high rpm position for better thrust control during landing. The engine flamed out and he could not make it to the airport. He was over the Yukon River, which was flowing with ice and there was no place to land. He immediately started the relight procedure, but it takes time to get that engine going from the feathered position. Just as the engine came to life again out of the feathered position, he was able to get full power just before stalling into the river on top of floating ice cakes. The parents at the airport saw this happening and were horrified at the sight of their children nearly crashing into the river.

Pratt and Whitney immediately grounded all the PT-6 airplanes and got on the problem. The combustion chamber and fuel control unit had to be redesigned to handle colder temperatures.

We lost one of the Astazou Porters before too long. Richard sent a new pilot up to Bettles to have the pilot there start training him in the airplane. The first thing the Bettles pilot did was put the new pilot in the left seat with a load of cargo and let him land it at Bear Creek with no dual controls, on a narrow runway with a bend in it. Not surprisingly, he totaled the airplane.

Then a Kotzebue pilot landed at Shungnak and reversed the prop without locking the tail wheel. The airplane ground looped into a ditch, knocked the gear off, bent the prop, and broke the right wing outboard of the wing strut attach point. Another pilot and I flew there with an FAA inspector and a replacement gear. We replaced the gear and inspected the prop. The prop was bent somewhat, but it ran up fine with no vibration. The big problem was the bent wing. It angled up about thirty degrees from the midpoint where the wing strut attached and you could move it up and down a couple of feet. I made the comment that if I flew it with full flap that there probably would not be much bending motion on the wing because the flap would be carrying most of the load. The FAA inspector said, "If you're stupid enough to try that, I guess I am stupid enough to let you." When I lifted off the ground I did not even have to hold any aileron pressure. I flew it to Kotzebue with full flaps and then the mechanic there found a nice, smooth pole that just fit in the wing, down through the lightening holes in the ribs, which kept the wing somewhat straight, allowing it to be flown with flaps up and it was ferried back to Fairbanks.

We had a similar situation with a Beaver. A pilot made a hard landing on a lake in a whiteout. The left gear broke and the wing was bent up at the same place as it had been on the Porter. Our mechanics went out and changed the gear. To temporarily repair the wing, they pulled down hard on it to straighten it out and then they wrapped a big sheet of aluminum around the broken area and held it in place with a lot of PK screws. They also hooked a cable from the wingtip to the landing gear wheel nut on the axle. When it was flown back to Fairbanks, a lot of people just shook their heads when they saw it.

FERRYING WRECKED AIRPLANES IN ALASKA HAD BEEN GOING on for a long time very safely. Those planes weren't airworthy to carry passengers but it wasn't considered risky flying. However, there was one circumstance where I did take some risk to save an airplane that I didn't have insured and couldn't afford to lose.

In 1962, my wife, Kathy, and I planned a trip to Denver in my Bonanza to visit her folks. I flew it to Seattle ahead of time to have the airplane striped and trimmed in red.

We departed Seattle on October 12, Columbus Day, for Vancouver, Washington, to visit with Kathy's uncle Jim. After landing at Vancouver, I set the brakes on the Bonanza and we caught a cab to Jim's apartment. After a little while I thought that I heard the wind blowing so I got up and walked out the door just in time to see a big tree uprooted and come crashing down. What a shock. I hollered inside and told Kathy that I was going to the airport. I managed to flag down a cab. The cab driver had a hard time getting to the airport because it seemed that every street he took was blocked by fallen trees. As we got close to the airport, I saw airplanes cartwheeling down the runway.

I was surprised to see the Bonanza where I parked it but it was turned about sixty degrees into the wind. The airplanes that had been parked in the same row were gone. I expected a good gust of wind to carry my plane away at any time so I quickly positioned myself on the leading edge of the right wing, which favored the wind a little. I was hoping that by lying on the wing lengthwise I might be able to kill enough lift to keep the airplane from blowing away. I sure did not want to lose that airplane because it was not insured.

I figured that if it looked like the airplane was going to fly away, I would just bail off the front of the wing. When a very strong gust moved the plane, I tried to roll off the leading edge but I discovered the wind was so strong that I was unable to do this. My only option was to get off the trailing edge but that course of action might take me with the airplane.

While I was lying on the wing, I watched a Navion fly up against the chains that were loosely tied to the wings of my plane. The Navion would leave the ground and when the chains caught it, it would dive back to the ground before leaping into the air again. When the wind was blowing the hardest, I heard an awful noise and looked to my right where there was a row of hangars. All the hangar doors had blown in, which caused the hangars to explode. The timbers and structural pieces blew away, just missing me, and then I saw the airplanes in the hangars fly up and away, some of them coming down upside down.

After I had been lying on the wing for about an hour, darkness fell. A woman drove by and asked if she could help in any way. I asked her if she had a rope and she said no, but she did have a garden hose in the trunk. I said that would work so when she got out the hose I hurriedly tied it on the upper part of the nose gear and then asked her to drive close to the nose of the airplane. I tied the other end of the hose to the front part of the chassis under the car and then I let the air out of the nose strut to reduce the angle of attack on the wing. I sat in the car with her with some peace of mind until the wind started to die down. I couldn't thank her enough. After about six hours at the airport, I was able to call Kathy to tell her that the airplane and I were OK.

It was later estimated that the wind had been as high as 120 knots. . . . The next morning the *Oregonian* newspaper had a photo of my Bonanza on the front page and the article said that it was the only airplane left standing after the storm. During what was later dubbed the Columbus Day Storm, I had been willing to risk my life to save that plane. I didn't tell Kathy what I had done, though. I didn't want to push my luck.

IN THE MID '60S, I ACCOMPANIED UNCLE SIG to the Paris Air Show to look at all the new airplanes being built in Europe. We were always looking for a better bush plane. One of the airplanes that we were interested in was the Max Holste 1521 Broussard. We arranged a flight and I had the opportunity to fly it with a demonstration pilot. Years later, I was browsing through some aviation books at a bookstore and I ran across two books written by an author whose name sounded familiar. It finally came to me that the author, Pierre Clostermann, had been the demonstration pilot in my flight in the Broussard. He was the most-decorated Free French ace of World War II. He is credited with flying 432 missions, shooting down 33 airplanes, and destroying 225 motor vehicles, 72 trains, and 5 tanks. Sure wish I had known that at the time.

The Alaska and Canadian bush continued to have a big demand for high-performance short field airplanes. Cessna quit building the Cessna 180 and 185 because tricycle-geared airplanes were easier to fly but the conventional gear was more adaptable to skis and thus pulls in a high price for used airplanes, especially in Alaska and Canada. It would not surprise me if they started to build the tail wheel airplanes again.

11

Ice Island Flying

In the early 1960s we were awarded the DEW Line contract again, after Alaska Airlines had had it for a while. They were operating a DC-4 from Fairbanks across the main DEW Line sites on the north coast. Wien Airlines leased the DC-4 from Alaska and I elected to fly it. I had fond memories of the DC-4 from my Pan Am days and I was glad to get down to the lower altitudes again. In addition to flying it on the DEW Line, we also used the DC-4 to supplement the F-27 scheduled flights when loads required a larger airplane.

In 1963, Arctic Research Laboratories (ARL), located at Point Barrow, was requesting bids to fly supplies and equipment to the ice islands north of Barrow. ARL was funded by the Navy Department for scientific work in the Arctic. We later learned that one of the things they were researching was the depth of the sea under the Arctic ice so they could use that information for nuclear submarines operating under the ice in the future. We still did not know whether there might be some land masses in the Arctic where the Russians might have established a base. I don't know how many trips Wien Airlines made to the islands—I made twenty flights myself—but at one time we had three crews based at Barrow for around-the-clock operations for quite a few days. Those trips were very challenging compared to our routine scheduled flights within Alaska but even though we had some trying experiences, we completed the contract successfully and it was lucrative for the airline.

The ice islands that ARL was using were created by glacier ice from large glaciers on Ellesmere Island in northern Canada. Glaciers flow like a river in very slow motion. As the face of a glacier calves into the ocean, the base of the glacier remains intact underwater and continues to move out into the ocean. Eventually, this large piece of ice goes so far out that buoyancy causes it to break off and float to the surface, creating an ice island. ARL could set up scientific stations on these large ice islands without fear of the surrounding pack ice crushing them.

The islands called T-3 and Arlis II in the Arctic Ocean, north of Point Barrow, were about 300 feet thick and three miles wide by five miles long. Most of their thickness was underwater so there was not much of a rise above the surface to distinguish them from the surrounding pack ice. They also were constantly drifting. For most of the time we were flying to them, T-3 was about 600 miles north of Point Barrow, the northernmost point in North America, and Arlis II was about 1,200 miles north, not too far from the North Pole.

The magnetic compass was not usable much farther north than Point Barrow. We had to use celestial navigation. Wien Airlines had an ex-Air France ground school instructor who was a very qualified celestial navigator. He went with us on a few trips to the ice islands to train us how to navigate celestially with a sextant and astrocompass and how to use grid navigation. We got to the point where we could do fairly well with the sextant with two star shots but when we tried three, the triangles on the map were very big. However, we were able to get close enough to pick up a 200-watt beacon from the ice islands and home in on it with our ADF receivers. This was tricky though because we had to get within about 200 miles from the station before we could pick up the beacon. One time the signal from the beacon was very weak and we did not pick it up until we were almost there. After identifying the signal, I turned the volume down but when I checked it again, the signal was gone and we were picking up music from a European radio station. We never did pick up the signal again so we had to turn around and go all the way back to Barrow. We later found out that a heavy ice storm had broken off the antenna at the island station.

One day when we were getting ready for another ice island trip from Barrow, we saw a beautiful shiny Navy DC-6 sitting on the ramp. The crew seemed to be interested in what we were doing and in our navigation system so we gave them a tour of the DC-4. We told them not to walk under the airplane because some dripping oil might ruin their nice uniforms. I showed them our astrocompass and I thought they would never stop laughing. Actually, I was pretty proud of it. I had carved a nice sharp piece of wood and attached it to the top of an old American Airlines computer with a Band-Aid. After aligning the zero degree mark to the nose of the airplane, we were able to get the relative bearing of the sun or a star by sighting down the wooden block. After checking the book on the sun or star and the time we were able to get a fairly accurate true heading, which we immediately set in the directional gyro. We had to keep doing this often because of the precession in the directional gyro.

We got a tour of the DC-6 and I have to admit, they had a real nice astrocompass and we did not have to worry about dripping oil under their plane.

WE FLEW THE TRIPS ON AND OFF THE year-round throughout 1963 and early 1964. It was challenging work with unpredictable and often extreme weather conditions. In the winter, it was pitch-dark twenty-four hours a day and landings were a real challenge. I think that it might have been a little like landing on a carrier at night except we had no glide slope reference and there were no surrounding lights to give some reference of a horizon. All we could see was two rows of lights out there somewhere in space and every time I made a correction to line up these rows of lights, the rows would appear to wander all over the windshield. I found it necessary to look at the instruments most of the time, with brief glances out the window at the lights for a quick reference until short final. I call them rows of lights but they were actually fire pots that the wind kept blowing out. The flares that stayed lit were few and far between.

Once when it was about 40 below with a 30-knot wind, we landed at Arlis II in the deep snow and could not taxi until we unloaded the cargo. When it is cold and the snow is deep, the snow gets into the brakes; the warm brakes melt the snow which then freezes, locking the wheels. This time, with the cold temperatures and wind, two of the shock struts along with the lock-out deboosters on the landing gears went flat, which meant we had no brakes. We were able to get one of the brakes dried out enough with the Herman Nelson heater so the wheel would turn but we still had no brakes. While trying to get the wheels and brakes working again, we also had to keep starting the engines to keep them warm. We were beginning to wonder if we would ever get the airplane off the ice.

We were able to get one wheel dried enough so that it would turn and not freeze up again and thought we better try to make the takeoff. I was able to taxi to the end of the strip. The other wheel did not rotate, which would give us some braking action at T-3 on our way back.

On the first takeoff attempt, the snow was so deep it prevented us from being able to lift the nose wheel and rotate for liftoff. I told the third pilot, who was sitting in the jump seat, to go back and get as much weight as possible to the tail of the airplane and have the passengers, ARL personnel, take the rear seats. On the next attempt, it was clear that, again, I would not be able to rotate so I asked the co-pilot in the right seat, Jim Williams, to help me bounce the nose wheel up and down with the elevator in hopes that the nose would bounce high enough to get some lift under the wing and continue to rotate. My big worry was breaking off the nose gear in the deep snow. The airplane was really taking a beating. We pushed and pulled hard on the control wheel and sure enough, the nose continued to rise and we became airborne.

We planned to stop at T-3 on our way back to Barrow because the runway there was hard-packed snow and they had more heaters and equipment we could use to try to get the brakes working and to get the right wheel to rotate. I did not want to land at Barrow with a locked wheel on the steel matted runway. We just had to hope that the frozen right wheel was still frozen and had not thawed when it was retracted in the wheel well so we could stop when we landed. Fortunately, the wheel was still locked and we landed safely at T-3. Once there, we got everything working again, except the landing gear struts, so we had brakes when we landed at Barrow.

Flying to the ice islands in summer brought its own challenges. In midsummer, the sun stayed at the same angle and it was daylight twenty-four hours a day. We were able to land on the plowed strip in the winter but as the sun got higher and higher, the melting ice and snow prevented us from landing. You could actually see small rivers of water flowing off the island. We then had to make the deliveries using airdrops.

These things were challenging enough, but on top of that we found that the weather and runway condition reports that we received from the ice island before every trip were not the most reliable. I don't think we ever got an unfavorable report.

Sometimes we would get there and let down as far as we dared with their reported altimeter setting and see nothing but clouds. After flying for about six hours, we made every effort to land, but safely. We would go down to about 200 feet and if we could see the shadows of snow and ice passing underneath through the clouds, we would then let down further. We could only do this in the daylight for airdrops. When we were to land at night, we flew over the camp, homing on the beacon at an altitude we felt was safe and then we would usually see the lights of the camp go by. We then were able to go a little lower for better forward visibility. They would always say that they just plowed the runway and it was in good condition but that was not always the case.

On one of the summer airdrop trips to T-3, the ceiling was down to about 150 feet, variable even though they had reported a much higher ceiling before we left Barrow. When we arrived they said the weather just moved in. We very carefully let down to a safe altitude until we saw the shadows of the pack ice underneath and then let down some more until we had the forward visibility we needed.

A few years earlier, the Air Force had crashed a Douglas C-47 at T-3 during a supply mission. As the years went by, the snow melted around the airplane but not in the shaded area underneath it. The airplane kept sitting higher and higher until it was precariously perched on a big, inverted snow cone. Approaching the radio beacon, we passed by the C-47 on its perch. We figured out the heading and time from the C-47 to the marked area where we were supposed to make the parachute drops. After passing the C-47 on the calculated heading I had to climb into the overcast before releasing the loads to give the parachutes enough altitude to open. To prevent stalling, I had to be careful how hard I rotated to climb. I usually felt a slight burble of a stall when I did this and they could feel it in the back. We made about five of these passes before finishing. When my co-pilot, Jim Williams, returned to the cockpit after helping to push the loads out, he reported that he almost went out with one load when his clothing got caught on a load that was rolling out of the plane.

When we ran into unexpected bad weather like this, it always caused us to remain on station longer while we tried to locate the drop zone. It was compounded by the fact that our estimated flight time was a big guess. We always knew the location of the islands from their reports, but there were no reports of winds aloft over the Arctic Ocean. Because of this unknown factor, we were often tempted to throw on another 200 or 300 gallons of fuel before leaving Point Barrow. Sometimes when we were sweating out having enough fuel to make it back to Point Barrow, I recalled two things. The first captain I flew with said, "These airplanes will fly overloaded but they will not fly without fuel." And common wisdom says, "The only time you have too much fuel is when you are on fire."

WHEN WE COULD NOT LAND ON THE ICE islands in the summer months, the scientists on the ice were stuck there. We knew that if they had a medical emergency in the summer, it would be a big problem. Sure enough, one summer one of their staff became very ill and they had to figure out a way to get him to a hospital.

Evergreen International Airlines had developed a personnel recovery system using their B-17. The way it worked was a long rope was hooked up to a harness on the person on the ground. The rope then was attached to a helium balloon that pulled the rope straight up in the air. The B-17 was fitted with a big V-shape structure extending forward from the nose of the airplane. The B-17 would fly into the rope just below the balloon and the rope would be clamped in the bottom of the V structure. As the airplane flew into the rope, the person would gradually be lifted off the ground and was soon trailing behind the B-17. A winch operator in the rear of the plane would clamp onto the rope and hook it up to a winch, and the person would be winched up and pulled through a rear entry.

When the report came in that a patient needed evacuation from Arlis II, ARL chartered the B-17 to fly to Barrow from Marana Air Base in Arizona and then all the way to Arlis II to do the pickup. When the B-17 arrived at Barrow, the sick person was advised of the plan to get him to a hospital, and he said, "Not me. No way, no how. That's too dangerous." So the B-17 had to fly all the way from Barrow back to Marana.

A short time later, the man died. The family insisted that the body be returned home. Since there was no further objection to the method of recovery, ARL chartered the B-17 to come back and recover the body. On the flight out to the island from Barrow, the B-17 encountered a lot of ice that also accumulated on the V truss work, which was not deiceable. They managed to do the recovery successfully but there was one more problem. After the man had died, the island personnel put his body in a space they dug in the ice in order to freeze him for preservation. The problem was that they had folded him over to save space so the winch operator in the plane was not able to pull the frozen body in through the plane's opening in that position. They had to leave the body hanging out of the airplane all the way to Barrow. Between ice accumulation and the additional drag of the body hanging out, the B-17 had to use more power for the return flight and landed at Barrow with minimum fuel.

OVERALL, THE ICE ISLAND FLYING CERTAINLY INCREASED MY flying experience. I loved flying the DC-4. It had a very comfortable and roomy cockpit and I was amazed how much of a beating it could take while landing on the Arlis II ice runway. Years later, when I was flying modern jet aircraft, I would have loved to be able to go back to flying the DC-4. The years of piston engine flying were the best of my flying career and with no hijackings to worry about or annoying TSA to boot. Also, flying the DC-4 taught me that no matter how much experience one might have, there is always more to learn.

On one flight in the DC-4 from Fairbanks to Barrow, we had a fire warning light on the number three engine. It often was a false indication but we never assumed that, so we feathered the engine. After landing at Barrow, our mechanic discovered that, sure enough, one of the cylinder heads had cracked causing hot gases to hit the detectors. Fairbanks asked me and co-pilot Don Gilbertson to do a three-engine ferry back to Fairbanks, which was a common practice without passengers. The takeoff went fine but when we leveled off at cruising altitude, the feathered number three propeller started to turn, ever so slowly. In time, the rpm increased to the point where we were building oil pressure. The oil pressure then supplied oil pressure to the propeller governor, which in turn started the unfeathering process. The worry then was would the propeller over-speed when it came out of feather with cold congealed oil. I elected to bring in the mixture control and turn the ignition switch on to get the oil warm enough to feather it again. I did not want to try feathering it with congealed oil because the thick oil could possibly cause it to unfeather instead of feather, which might cause a runaway prop. We thought about returning to Barrow but the weather had deteriorated to below minimums and I did not want to make a below minimums three-engine approach so we continued this drill several times before landing at Fairbanks.

We later found out that we were supposed to stuff a rope into the number one cylinder spark plug hole to prevent the piston from moving up. I'm not sure that our maintenance people were aware of this trick either. Lesson learned.

Flying to such remote locations forced us to be fairly self-sufficient. Even after landing, we sometimes had severe conditions to deal with. Sometimes the runways on Arlis II and T-3 would not harden after plowing, preventing us from taxiing to the unloading area. One time after landing on T-3, we were moving very slowly, trying to make it to the unloading area with full power when the number three engine started backfiring. We had to shut down there and look for the problem. My co-pilot, Joe Cross, was also a very good mechanic. He went to work on the engine and when the cowling was off, he found an intake pipe that had blown away from the cylinder. He reinstalled the pipe and that fixed the problem. He was wearing a brand-new parka and it was covered with dirty black engine oil. He turned the cleaning bill into the company and they refused to pay it. Just imagine what it would have cost to fly a mechanic almost all the way to the North Pole. . . .

WHEN ANOTHER OPERATOR WAS AWARDED THE DEW LINE contract Wien Airlines turned the DC-4 back to Alaska Airlines, but we thought that we needed to acquire a four engine airplane to continue to do ice island flying and to supplement the scheduled routes when cargo and passenger loads necessitated a bigger airplane.

We considered both the DC-6 and the Lockheed Constellation and ended up leasing, and later buying, a Lockheed L-749 Constellation, known as the Connie. Pacific Northern Airlines (PNA) was contracted to train about five of the Wien crews. My instructor at PNA was the legendary Frank Hansen. We had some work done on the plane, including the addition of a large cargo door, before I ferried it to Fairbanks with Don Gilbertson, a Wien pilot, and a PNA flight engineer. Wien had hired two furloughed PNA flight engineers until we could train our own. Bob Carpenter was our first engineer and I think he could have built a Connie from scratch.

Shortly after we arrived at Fairbanks with the Connie, the FAA passed new regulations for scheduled airlines. This required creating training manuals and operations manuals, proving emergency evacuation capability, fulfilling inspection requirements, and much more. When the weight of the paperwork and the weight of the airplane were the same, we were able to begin operations. The Connie turned out to be very expensive for us to operate. PNA had good luck with the Connie because they standardized in one airplane and had good utilization. It is cheaper to operate one type of airplane than several different types. That was very difficult for Wien Airlines to do because of the varied requirements of our service.

When we finally began operations with the Connie, we used it on our scheduled runs and for more ice island flying; however, we only did airdrops on the ice islands because we did not think that the nose gear would stand up to the deep snow and rough conditions on the islands.

One of our first trips to the islands with the Connie was an airdrop to Arlis II. As always, we tried to pad the fuel enough for unexpected winds. For the first trip with the Connie, we had onboard three of the senior Wien captains: Bill English, Tom Richards, and myself and co-pilot Jim Williams. We were able to complete the airdrop successfully and we headed back to Barrow. On the way we learned that the Barrow weather had deteriorated to below our landing minimums. When we heard that we probably would not be able to land at Barrow, we started figuring out ways to save fuel. We were aware that the Connie engines had a spark advance position that would give us better fuel consumption. When we were trained at PNA they told us they never used it and so we never learned how. We got out the manuals and followed the procedure to shift to spark advance. The airplane was equipped with fuel flow instruments so we noticed right away that this reduced our fuel consumption. When we arrived at Barrow the weather was still bad so we continued to our alternate destination, Umiat. As we approached Umiat, the weather there closed in so we continued to Bettles. Again, the weather closed in there so our only choice was to see if we could make it to Fairbanks. Since Bill and Tommy were up front on duty, I decided to go to the rear of the airplane as far as I could because generally the rear of an airplane is safer during a crash landing. After landing I went up front and noticed that all the gas gauges were reading zero or slightly above. Our flight time was 17 hours 21 minutes.

Three days later, I was scheduled to take the Connie on a scheduled passenger flight to Nome and Kotzebue. The procedure on takeoff was for the captain to turn around and look at the BMEP gauges at 80 knots to confirm that takeoff power was holding. These gauges were an indication of the actual power the engines were producing. When I looked at the gauges at 80 knots, I saw that all four of the needles were unwinding. I couldn't believe my eyes. I hesitated for a second or two and when I detected a change in the sound of the engines, I wiped the power off since I still had room to stop. The engineer had not been looking at the torque meters so when I pulled the power off, he turned around and said, "What happened?"

I taxied back to the run-up area and ran up the engines again, one at a time. Sure enough, shortly after reaching takeoff power, the engines started to backfire. I taxied back to the terminal and we unloaded the passengers.

We went back to the run-up area and kept running the engines to takeoff power until they finally continued to run normally. All this time the mechanics were scouring every manual to find a clue to what the problem might be. We finally found the answer. The only fuel that ARL had was 115/145 fuel. Normal fuel for the Connie was 100/130 octane. If 115/145 octane fuel was used, it was necessary to increase power to METO (maximum except takeoff) power every hour for a minute to burn off the lead deposits on the spark plugs. Since we were using a low cruise control power setting, the cylinders ran cooler than normal and created deposits inside the cylinders, which had caused detonation on the next takeoff. Another lesson learned.

I enjoyed flying the Connie but it was not a moneymaker for the airline. We only made the one airdrop trip to the ice islands with the Connie. Then another operator was contracted to use the Lockheed C-130, which could carry bigger loads for ice island support. After about two years of operation, and only about 2,000 hours, Wien retired the Connie and put it up for sale. It sat for two years and was finally sold for $25,000 with the belly pack full of parts and I ferried it to Seattle.

12

From the Turboprop to the Jet Age

In 1959, Wien Alaska Airlines bought their first turboprop airliner, a Fairchild F-27, one of two with more to come. I was thrilled to be able to fly high and fast but in time I began to miss flying through the mountains looking at the wildlife and enjoying the beauty of the country, as I could do when I flew the piston powered planes. I still frequently flew the bush planes, which helped, but I never enjoyed flying the F-27 as much as the earlier planes.

Even so, the F-27 turned out to be a good airplane for us during that time. The only recurring problem we had was that sometimes in the cold weather, the pneumatic system would freeze up and we could not get the gear up. The gear, brakes, and nose wheel steering were pneumatic instead of hydraulic. This was common with many foreign designed airplanes. The F-27 was originally a Fokker design, and Fairchild had acquired the rights to build them in this country.

When moisture collected in the pneumatic system, the lines would freeze and the pneumatic pumps would not build up pressure in the reservoir. Sometimes, if the gear would not quite go all the way up, we would advise the passengers that there would be a little bump and we would push the wheel forward to less than one G and the gear would come up and lock. One time we were very low on pneumatic pressure and I kept trying with more and more forward push. Eventually I unintentionally went less than zero gravity. The portable biffy in the lavatory lifted out of the container and spilled all over the floor.

When I was advised of the situation by the flight attendant, I went back with a lot of rags and paper towels and started trying to wipe up the mess. The smell was one thing but the more we wiped, the more sudsy the mess got. The chemical solution in the can made a lot of suds when wiped. That went on the list of one of the most embarrassing moments in my life. However, the gear did come up.

Not too long after we acquired our second F-27, I was asked to do a late night test flight on our first F-27 to check out a problem with the propeller operation. I had been flying all day and was very tired but my doing it would save calling out another pilot just to do the test hop.

For many years we had ferried airplanes and had done test hops without a certified co-pilot, which was within regulations back then. This time, a mechanic rode along in the co-pilot's seat to monitor the propeller. He happened also to be a private pilot and I guess that night he decided to be a co-pilot instead of a mechanic. As we were accelerating down the runway, I noticed a red light come on in the cockpit. I looked over to the right side and saw that the gear handle was in the up position with the red light shinning in the gear handle. I couldn't believe what I was seeing, but I instinctively hauled back on the wheel just as the landing gear was retracting. As we rotated I felt the rear of the fuselage thump on the runway. I was just stunned that the mechanic had thought that we were airborne and had pulled the gear handle to the up position. The propeller worked fine during the test flight but the bottom of the rear fuselage was badly damaged. This was very costly for the airline because the tourist season was just beginning and it was about two months before repairs were completed. This meant we had just the one F-27 in service when we had counted on two for that year.

After the flight, all I could think about was how nice it would be if I could just backtrack a few minutes and start over. The FAA called it an incident and I was not blamed, but Uncle Sig held me responsible. I should have briefed the mechanic to just sit on his hands, just as captains did with new co-pilots in the early days before cockpit resource management (CRM). CRM, which assigns the first officer (called co-pilots then) more responsibility and duties, such as reading checklists, verifying movements, doing the radio transmissions, tuning and verifying frequency selection, and speaking up about any concerns he might have, has become key to modern day crew training. I would have been better off with no one in the seat unless he was a trained co-pilot who would have known we were not airborne yet. And even a trained co-pilot knows to never pull up the gear without the captain's command.

WHILE MUCH OF MY WORK WAS FAIRLY ROUTINE in those years, or as routine as things get in Alaska, there were some pretty memorable events. I once had Ted Kennedy on one of my flights. He was touring Alaska, campaigning for his brother John. We had a nice conversation on the ramp before departing Kotzebue and he seemed to be interested in my thoughts about Alaska's problems. A few years later, I flew a charter flight taking Robert Kennedy, along with famous mountaineers Jim Whittaker and Bradford Washburn, to Whitehorse. Robert wanted to climb Mount Kennedy, which recently had been named in honor of JFK. He wasn't nearly as friendly as Ted. I invited him to come to the cockpit before we departed Juneau but I was unsuccessful in engaging in any kind of conversation. He just kept trying to get his hair back in place. Both Jim Whittaker and Bradford Washburn were very friendly.

On another of our scheduled flights to Point Barrow, the station manager informed me that actor Cliff Robertson would be on our flight returning to Fairbanks. My first thought was, *Wow!* He was a hero of mine. He and actress Dina Merrill had been in the Arctic, doing some filming about polar bear hunting. We had a nice talk in the terminal and after takeoff, I asked him if he would like to come to the cockpit. I don't think that Dina Merrill wanted him to leave her in the cabin but he came to the cockpit anyway and kept us entertained for about an hour. He told us a hilarious story about a balloon race he had recently been in with his friend and famous movie stunt pilot Frank Tallman. The race was from Catalina Island to the mainland and it was a harrowing experience. They had trouble adjusting the heat from the torches to maintain elevation and ended up flying either too high or too low, dragging the basket in the water. Cliff had us laughing hysterically, especially when he told us Tallman's admission that he had been flying for forty years and only discovered that he was afraid of heights as he was lying on the bottom of the balloon's basket.

When the massive 1964 earthquake hit Alaska, I was sitting in the airport barbershop in Fairbanks getting a haircut when the fluorescent lights started swinging. The building was swaying very gently. At first, there was no contact with Anchorage but eventually bits of information started coming in.

Lowell Thomas Jr. landed in Fairbanks in his 180 just after the earthquake and I told him what had happened A few hours later we prepared an F-27 to go to Anchorage with the Fairbanks mayor and a load of doctors. Lowell was worried about his family in Anchorage so he flew back with us. When we arrived over Anchorage it looked like a ghost town. There were no lights anywhere and the whole area was fogged in. The tower at Anchorage International had fallen over and there were reports that the runway was damaged. We tried to find Merrill Field through breaks in the fog but there was not enough visibility in the moonlight to accomplish a landing. We were able to make a ground control approach at Elmendorf AFB because they were operating on standby power. The Air Force provided us with a bus that drove slowly through the fog. We did not see much on the bus ride but we found out that most of the damage was in the neighborhood that Lowell's family lived in and also in downtown Anchorage. The area where the Thomases lived had a slippery clay formation one layer below ground and the whole neighborhood just slipped down into the Cook Inlet area as if on a plate of grease. Once we got into Anchorage, we learned that Lowell's home had been destroyed, but he located his family at a nearby church. Two of their neighbors' children had fallen into an open crevasse and disappeared. Unlike the time during the flood, there wasn't much I could do to assist and so I soon returned to Fairbanks.

Wien Air Alaska grew steadily throughout the 1960s. In 1968, Wien merged with Northern Consolidated Airlines and Ray Peterson, the former president and CEO of Northern Consolidated, soon became the new head of the airline. Sig continued as a director, as did my father. The merged airline was called Wien Consolidated Airlines for a while but the name was eventually changed back to Wien Air Alaska. The merger was the right thing to do but as with most mergers, we were plagued with internal adjustments and seniority problems. It marked the beginning of a period when service to many of the smaller communities was cancelled. Smaller air taxi operators then picked up this work, stimulating their growth and numbers.

Before the merger with Northern Consolidated, I accepted the job as chief pilot and, later, director of flight operations for the airline. I hated sitting at a desk though as it turned out, I continued to fly almost as much as I did as a line pilot on top of my desk duties. I actually took a pay cut for this position. I lasted about two years before I was able to find a qualified replacement. I will say I learned a lot about human relations in those two years. During that time I also briefly became acting chief stewardess by default because as director of flight operations I found it necessary to relieve our chief stewardess. As chief stewardess I found out that I am totally defenseless against tears.

I flew the F-27 for about ten years before the airline started buying Boeing 737s and we officially entered the jet age. In 1969, Wien ordered their first Boeing 737, leasing N461GB until the Boeing orders came through. I was trained at Pacific Southwest Airlines and from this time on, my airline flying became more routine although the helicopter flying I was doing with Merric during the same period provided me with more than enough adventure. By this point, we had two more children in addition to Kim: Kurt, born in 1963 and Kent, born in 1969.

The 737s that Wien and Consolidated first ordered, just before the merger, were equipped with a gravel kit. There were still many gravel runways in Alaska, mostly in the northern areas, which necessitated the installation of the gravel kit. The modification involved a ski shaped, rectangular platform located a few inches off the runway and mounted just behind the nose wheel. This kept the spray of gravel low so the rocks did not fly up into the engines. Additionally, a tube was mounted on the lower nose engine cowl pointing forward and down at a forty-five-degree angle with three tubes mounted on the end pointing rearward blowing bleed air from the engines. This force of air kept gravel from rising up in little whirlpools and then being sucked into the engines. Boeing experimented with different versions of a gravel kit before settling on this very effective system. Later deliveries of the 737, after most of the runways were paved, did not have the ski but both Wien and Boeing found that the blow tubes on the engines were very effective in reducing foreign object digestion, even from a paved runway.

Before the merger, another modification to the 737s that Wien requested was a "combi" configuration. With this setup, the bulkhead between the passenger seating and the cargo area could be moved forward and backward depending on the number of passengers and amount of cargo. In the cargo area, either passenger seats mounted on platforms or cargo containers, called igloos, could be rolled into the plane on ball bearing–type rollers and locked into position. This allowed for an all-passenger configuration, with those seats being slightly elevated due to the rollers underneath.

The 737 was a great airplane for Alaska operations, especially with the gravel kit and combo configuration. While jet flying made things more routine for me, I did have some heart-pounding moments. After one passenger flight to Nome, we were returning to Anchorage on a cargo-only flight with first officer Gary Gale. An igloo cargo container full of empty propane bottles was loaded at Nome for refilling at Anchorage. Before the bottles were placed onboard, the valves were supposed to be opened for a while and then closed, with additional plugs inserted in the openings. I asked the station manager if this had been done and he assured me that it had been. In reality, the valves had been opened but weren't then closed and no plugs had been installed. When we took off, our flight attendant called on the interphone and said there was a propane smell in the back of the plane. We soon smelled it too and it got very bad in a hurry. We turned around right away and I told the flight attendant to come forward and bring her portable oxygen bottle and we put on our portable masks as well. By the time we landed back at Nome our oxygen bottles had almost expired and we opened the windows immediately after depressurization. Needles to say, I was one unhappy aviator.

Another time on a scheduled passenger flight between Anchorage and Fairbanks, we had a cargo igloo full of Herman Nelson heaters that were to be overhauled at Fairbanks. The gasoline in the tanks was supposed to be totally emptied out before loading. It turned out that the tanks were not drained and the heaters were stacked on end for space considerations. When the Boeing rotated on takeoff, gasoline gurgled out past the gas caps and flowed out of the igloo and down the passenger aisle. The flight attendant notified us of the fumes and my first thought was that they were caused by the decrease in cabin pressure, allowing the fumes to flow into the cabin. I immediately lowered the cabin altitude and leveled the airplane at the present altitude.

By the time I realized what had actually happened, we were more than halfway to Fairbanks. There was such a strong gasoline smell that I hated to even key the mike for fear of an electrical spark somehow causing an explosion. Fortunately we landed without incident but it took a long time to get the gasoline smell out of the airplane. In addition to one unhappy aviator, this time we also had a lot of unhappy passengers.

ON OCTOBER 18, 1971, A WIEN FLIGHT FROM Anchorage to Bethel was hijacked at gunpoint. I wasn't on that flight but it was a tense day for everyone at Wien. Captain Don Peterson, First Officer Ray Miller, and Second Officer Keith Forsgren were the pilots. Margie Hertz was the lead flight attendant and one of the other flight attendants, Nancy Davis, was on her first flight with the airline. The passengers and Margie Hertz were released when the plane returned to Anchorage for fuel and it all ended peacefully when Nancy Davis was able to talk the hijacker into giving up. Several hours later the airplane reversed course with the crew safe, in Vancouver, British Columbia. Around this time it seemed that hijackings were happening more frequently. We hadn't been particularly worried about it before, but after it happened at Wien, we were all much more concerned about being hijacked.

I HAD LOOKED FORWARD TO FLYING THE JET airliners but it wasn't long before I wanted to be back in the DC-4, C-46, or the Connie. In addition to having to fly at higher altitudes, I found that the jets simply were not as interesting to fly. When you start a jet engine, it is somewhat like turning on a vacuum cleaner. There's the flip of a switch followed by a humming sound. Starting a big piston engine takes finesse and is followed by a wonderful sound of barking, popping, snorting, throbbing, and backfires with smoke, culminating in the sound of many engine parts trying hard to put out some horsepower. You can take pride in learning how to start the big reciprocating engines with the minimum of backfires. I suppose some of it was simply resisting change as I got older but the profession was also changing away from the seat of the pants flying that I loved, to one that required more flying by the numbers with a lot more regulations and restrictions. I was finding that it simply wasn't the profession it used to be. If I can't be in the cockpit, I like the jets better as a passenger.

13

Turbulence for Wien Air Alaska

The 1979 pilots' strike against Wien Air Alaska is a hard part of my life to write about. An employee labor strike can be a very emotional experience for employees and families because there is such a vast difference of opinion within a labor union as to how to handle management/labor conflicts. Longtime friends can become enemies forever. I do not want to bring up old wounds or stir up any more controversy but I feel that I should address this period of time to the best of my memory since it encompassed a major setback in my life.

During the days of piston powered airliners, the FAA required a flight engineer on aircraft with gross weight over 80,000 pounds. The Airline Pilots Association (ALPA) agreed with the thinking that piston powered airplanes over 80,000 pounds were too complicated for only two pilots, so a flight engineer was required to handle much of the workload. However, with the advent of the jet engine, airliners became much less complicated though they had higher gross weights. So although the Boeing 737 weighed more than 80,000 pounds, it was certificated for a two-pilot crew. Now ALPA's reasoning for continuing to require a three-pilot crew changed to needing more eyes in the cockpit to look for traffic. That had never been mentioned by ALPA before. It appeared that they just wanted the third man in the cockpit regardless of the reason. I couldn't help but wonder why three sets of eyes was not a concern before in two-pilot piston airplanes under 80,000 pounds.

My experience in the 737 was that the third pilot was always in the way in the jump seat and had no important duties that the two pilots could not do. It seemed to me that he added to more unrelated conversation in the cockpit, thus becoming more of a distraction and actually reducing the safety factor. Whether the third pilot can realistically be considered a safety enhancement or a featherbedding position is a subject for unlimited discussion.

ALPA, however, decided to hold the line using Wien Airlines and pushed for the Wien pilots to strike. We were picked to be the sacrificial lamb. The strike began in May 1977 but it was a lost cause from the beginning. Boeing had already received the FAA approval for the two-pilot Boeing 767 that was being built and, while the Wien pilots went on strike, Frontier Airlines was flying with a two-pilot contract.

ALPA can be very proud that they have been instrumental in airline safety throughout the years. But I think that somewhere along the way, membership numbers became the overriding priority and they lost sight of what was in the best interests of the pilots and the airlines. ALPA and the Wien pilot group didn't seem to understand that no matter how damaging the strike might be to the airline, it was likely that management would never hire the pilots back, regardless of the cost. The matter of principle, or even vindication, sometimes dictates the course of action, not economics. This was certainly the case with Wien Air Alaska management. It was a fallacy to think that the pilots were irreplaceable.

I did not want to cross the picket line and turn against my friends, and I didn't, but I think my conscience paid the price. My father pioneered Wien Alaska Airlines so I was torn between my deep roots in the company and my allegiance to my fellow pilots. It was the most difficult decision I ever made. One pilot I knew who had grown up with his dad's airline, which was eventually merged into Northern Consolidated Airlines before it merged with Wien, could not, in good conscience, honor the strike. He lost many friends and his warehouse was set on fire. Other senior pilots felt that it was a terrible mistake to turn against the company that gave them their big chance for a great career. They honored the strike but were against it from the beginning.

While most of the striking pilots were deeply angry at the replacement pilots, some were unable to hold them to blame. We walked off the job during a time when there were many qualified pilots looking for work and we left vacancies to be filled. It would be asking a lot to expect out-of-work pilots to not take advantage of an employment opportunity, especially when most people thought our cause was so ridiculous. The general perception was that the strike was primarily a featherbedding issue. I personally did not hold any grudge against the replacement pilots. I did, however, have a grudge against one striking pilot. He was not one who struggled with his conscience. He was a strong supporter of striking and was very vocal about it in the union meetings. However, when he realized that maybe we would not be able to go back to work, he suddenly was back flying the line with the replacement pilots.

During the strike I flew a C-46 for the Ball brothers at Dillingham, hauling fish from Togiak to Dillingham and sometimes on to Anchorage to the fish processing facility there. At least there was one pretty good side benefit to this: I was back flying the airplane that I had missed flying all those years.

On one flight, Jerry Ball, one of the owners, said, "When you get to Anchorage, grab yourself a fish." I picked out the biggest one I could find and when I got home, I put it on my scale and it weighed in at seventy pounds. I cut the fish up into thick steaks and we had fresh salmon for dinner that night and many more.

I had to do something to receive strike benefits and I could not possibly carry a picket sign, so instead I flew a Beechcraft Baron for ALPA to cover the state for support for the strike. There understandably was little support from citizens in Alaska who thought that we were putting a crimp in the airlines' service to the communities.

On one flight for ALPA we headed for the northern part of Alaska in the Beech Baron to solicit support for the strike. After landing at several villages on the Arctic coast, we departed Point Hope for Kotzebue after dark. Our last refueling was at Umiat, on the Colville River. Earlier reports showed good conditions over our entire route. But when we contacted Kotzebue radio after leaving Point Hope, they reported the Kotzebue weather as sky obscured, one-sixteenth-mile visibility, blowing snow, and wind out of the east at 40 knots. So much for weather forecasts. We initially had enough fuel to go to Nome but with the unforecast strong winds out of the south, Nome was not within our reach and neither was Galena. The only thing that we could do was land at Kotzebue, one way or the other. By the time we got there, it had been dark for several hours. I flew over the airport and could see the lights of the runway straight down. I thought the landing would not be a problem because, fortunately, the 40-knot wind was right down the runway. Onboard were two other Wien captains—Jim Freericks and Tom Richards. I turned on the landing lights and did a tight 360-degree overhead approach. As soon as I turned final there was no runway to be seen. The landing lights just lit up the snow in front of us and blocked any view of the runway lights. That wasn't going to work so I turned off the landing lights and immediately saw the runway lights again as I was looking straight down. But as I turned final, the runway was again not visible. Just as in ice fog, you can see straight down, but as soon as you try to see the runway at an angle, the slant distance through the blowing snow is too great for visual reference.

I thought, *Oh boy. Another fine fix I've got myself into.*

The only option was to do the instrument landing system (ILS) all the way to the runway in hopes of seeing the lights at the last minute. I descended as low as I dared on the ILS and made a go-around. Jim said, "I wish I could be of some help." Tommy got out of the middle seat and got as far back as he could in case we crashed. After capturing the glide slope on the second attempt, I reduced airspeed so as to be at the right attitude for touchdown. If we were flying at a normal ILS speed, as I did on the first ILS, the nose wheel would hit first and we would just bounce back into the air. With the low approach speed and the 40-knot headwind, we were coming down the glide slope very slowly, with a ground speed of about 45 knots, which made the descent rate only about 250 feet per minute. I was working hard to keep the needles centered and did not look out. I told Jim to let me know if he saw the runway lights. I did not look out until I felt the touchdown. It rolled on about the same as a normal landing. I am sure the snow on the runway helped. As we were rolling out, Jim said he saw a light go by. That was the first light we saw. What a relief.

It took us awhile to find the ramp. The FAA flight service station agent did not report us for landing below minimums. I think our good friend Marge Baker, who had built Baker Air Service into a very successful airline after her husband's death, talked him out of it.

Years before when we were doing six-month checks in Fairbanks in the F-27, I suggested that we try doing an ILS all the way to touchdown in case we should ever find ourselves in that situation. With one pilot under the hood and the other check pilot monitoring, we were able to accomplish some decent landings. I think that helped a lot for this zero-zero landing at Kotzebue.

THE NATIONAL LABOR RELATIONS BOARD CLOSED THE CASE and it looked as though we would never be able to go back to work. If it had not been for a few of our pilots who took it upon themselves to get congressional help, the pilots would never have gone back to work. Alaska Representative Don Young was a major force credited for getting a bill attached to the deregulation bill in 1978 requiring the formation of a fact-finding commission to study the strike and make a recommendation. ALPA was not in favor of this course of action and insisted that we not go this route. But those few pilots did it anyway. The recommendation from the commission was to put the Wien pilots back to work and the strike ended in March 1979. The airline was not obligated to abide by the recommendation, but some legislators made it clear to Jim Flood, who was president of the airline by that time, that if they did not, it would not go well for them in the future.

After the strike was over, ALPA did their best to take credit for ending the strike. It should also be noted that ALPA did not poll any of the ALPA members from other airlines about whether or not they would support a paycheck deduction to fund the salaries of Wien pilots during the strike. We later became aware that a lot of the pilots were unhappy with the paycheck deduction.

The strike was a very unhappy and stressful time for me. Longtime friendships were strained and the goodwill that my dad and uncle had strived to create throughout the years was compromised. The company had already begun to change after the merger when Ray Peterson became CEO and there had been much unrest between pilots and management. This may have contributed to allowing ALPA to push us into striking. It was not a great moment for ALPA, either. I heard indirectly that the ALPA management in later years considered their handling of the third pilot issue and the resulting Wien strike a huge mistake and a dark period in their history. And it sure was.

A whole book can be written about the last years of a once respected, proud, and pioneering airline. After Ray Peterson became CEO, the Wien influence was minimized. In 1980, as the Wien family involvement in the airline diminished, Household Finance bought all the outstanding stock. That was the first time that the original investors were able to realize any return on investment. In the early years, I don't think that my dad ever drew more than a $500 monthly salary. Any surplus went back into the company. He paid his pilots $500 a month plus a commission of the revenue they flew. His pilots often made more than he did, sometimes double. In the public's view, the Wien name represented service to Alaska and that was always the primary goal.

The merger was the right thing to do at the time because both my dad and Sig had essentially retired, though they both remained on the board of directors. My life was changing as well. My wife, Kathy, and I decided to divorce and we congenially dissolved our marriage. During the last few years of Wien Air Alaska, I was transferred to Seattle, when Wien expanded their route structure to many of the western states necessitating a crew base there. I bought a house on an airpark in Kent and I loved being able to walk out of the kitchen into my hangar.

The 1978 deregulation legislation had taken the industry from extreme regulation to extreme deregulation. Before deregulation, decisions about routes and rates took years to decide and many of the routes were awarded as a result of political influence. For example, part of the reason for the demise of Pan American World Airways was due to the fact that Pan American fell in political disfavor with the executive branch and so did not get approval for domestic routes they badly needed to support the international routes they pioneered. They were only able to gain some domestic routes by merging with National Airlines in 1980. At the same time, other American and foreign carriers were granted routes in competition with Pan American's overseas routes.

After deregulation, airlines could fly anywhere and rates were all over the place. It became more difficult for high cost, union airlines to compete with upstart nonunion airlines that hired furloughed pilots off the street at much lower salaries and benefits. Unions said that it was a management problem and management said that the costs had to be reduced in order to compete.

By around 1983, Household Finance had become somewhat disenchanted with their investment in Wien. Wien Airlines never generated enough earnings to justify dividends for stockholders but the airline continued to increase in value by reinvesting in equipment, airplanes, and ground facilities, which did not seem to affect stock value.

Neil Bergt, owner of Alaska International Air, made an offer to buy Wien from Household Finance and then negotiated to merge the airline into Western Airlines in return for a greater value in Western stock. This would have saved thousands of Wien jobs and would have helped to prop up Western, which was on the verge of bankruptcy. The Civil Aeronautics Board (CAB) was still in effect then and their approval hinged on Neil divesting himself from any control over his cash cow, Alaska International Air, supposedly to avoid a conflict of interest. Of course, Neil was not going to do that so that was the end of that. A few months later, CAB was deactivated by the deregulation bill. By that time the proposed merger would not have been a problem because after deregulation the rule that airlines could not have ownership in more than 5 percent of another airline was eliminated. This created a great deal of turbulence in the industry as individuals were also able to manipulate leveraged buyouts and liquidation until some additional legislation could be passed.

Under the ownership of Household Finance, James Flood continued to be president of the airline. As president, Mr. Flood knew the shares of stock were grossly undervalued. The stock was selling for about $6 a share and the liquidation value was about $12 a share. Knowing the value of the company, he was able to work with the bank on a leveraged buyout using the airline as collateral. Household Finance agreed to sell the airline to Mr. Flood, putting him in a very good financial position.

In November 1984, James Flood announced a temporary shutdown of Wien Air Alaska for thirty days to reorganize under chapter 11. Of course, operations were never renewed. All employees were laid off, assets sold or leased, and Mr. Flood made millions without the continued headache of running an airline that had increasing union problems. What a shame that some of the original investors could not have realized a profit.

I am glad that my father, who died in 1977, did not witness this tragic end of the historic airline he devoted so much of his life to.

There are those who feel Mr. Flood intended from the beginning to liquidate the airline. Whether he did or did not, the pilots' strike helped facilitate his shutting down the airline and selling off the assets. The efforts by ALPA and the pilot group played right into James Flood's hands. It had a lot to do with James Flood becoming president. Ray Peterson would never have liquidated the airline. James Flood had the support of the bankers and the business community because they did not support the strike. In the end, Mr. Flood received an award for his business accomplishment, while more than a thousand employees were put on the street.

Here I am in the cockpit of the Boeing 737.

Me and cousin Captain Bob Wien, son of Ralph Wien, killed at Kotzebue, Alaska, in 1930. We are getting ready to depart Fairbanks for Wien Airlines inaugural service to Seattle.

Visiting General James H. Doolittle in Carmel, California, in 1987 on my way to Los Angeles to start working for Total Air flying Lockheed 1011s. He was ninety years old at the time.

Bill Anders (an oustanding formation pilot) on my left wing during a formation flight. *Photo © Lyle Jansma.*

Getting ready to go on tour with CAF B-29.

Me with the Boeing Stearman I used to own.

A photo taken in Chino, California, of the Lockheed P-38 that Richard and I had for a short time.

Bob Robbins, sitting on the left, was the experimental Boeing B-29 test pilot who succeeded famed test pilot Eddie Allen after he was killed. Bob liked to tour with us in *FIFI* and help with cockpit tours. Bob was a textbook of information and was very helpful to me.

14

Life After Wien Air Alaska

A few months after Wien Airlines was liquidated, Joe Soloy asked if I would be interested in helping him sell the Cessna conversions his company had engineered, converting the piston engines to turboprop conversions. So I went to work for Joe Soloy as a demonstration pilot, test pilot, and salesman for the Soloy Corporation in Olympia, Washington. In 1985, I remarried and soon after that, my new wife, Barbara, and I flew a turboprop Soloy Cessna 207 to Alaska on a demonstration tour. One of the people I demonstrated the airplane to was my good friend Lowell Thomas Jr. He ended up buying a Soloy 207 for his Talkeetna operation. When he later sold his air service, he retained the 207 and used it to provide sightseeing flights around Mount McKinley for the guests at Wally and Jerri Cole's Camp Denali and the North Face Lodge near Wonder Lake. Lowell was very familiar with the mountain and he knew the name of every peak and glacier in and around it as well as the history of all the early climbing expeditions. Those flights, which took off from an old mining strip called Kantishna, were very popular with the guests.

In January 1987 I was offered a job flying Lockheed 1011s for a small company called Total Air, which had been formed by a group of Braniff pilots after Braniff went out of business. The primary mission for Total Air was to support a travel agency called Trans Ocean Travel and Leisure, thus the name, Total Air. The job paid more and provided more steady work than my job with Joe Soloy so I took it; however, the long and irregular hours it required eventually took a toll on me.

My neighbor Fred Ellsworth and I drove to Los Angeles where I started training in the 1011. On the way, I called General Jimmy Doolittle in Carmel to see if we could stop by for a visit. The general and his wife, Jo, were longtime friends of my parents. We had a nice visit with him and enjoyed asking him questions such as what was the worst airplane he ever flew and what was the best. He said the worst was the Gee Bee and the best was the Spitfire. He said the Gee Bee wanted to tumble going around the pylons.

I told him that I was restoring a B-25 and I planned to paint it just like the B-25 he flew on the Tokyo raid. I asked him if he would go flying with me in the B-25 but he replied, "Thank you but when I turned sixty years old, I decided I would never fly an airplane again." I guess he figured that he had pushed his luck as far as he dared. I consider Jimmy Doolittle to be one of the greatest pilots of all time. He was the first graduate at MIT in aeronautical engineering so he not only knew how to fly but he knew how airplanes were built and what made them fly. He is also one of the most humble men I have ever had the privilege to know.

The 1011 was a great airplane and I loved flying it. I had long since decided that I was too old to learn how to use a computer but I was forced into it at Total Air because the flight management system (FMS) was all computerized. On my first trip with chief check pilot Rod Boone, he was trying to explain to me all the workings of the navigation system. I was hoping that the system would just go up in smoke so I could revert to manual tuning of the VORs (navigation system). The next thing I knew, the system had become inoperative and Rod was spouting a few expletives. I thought it best not to tell him that my prayers had been answered. However, after I had some hands-on experience and became more familiar with the FMS, I loved it. I flew as first officer for about a year and a half before being checked out as captain.

Much of the work I did for Total Air was flying military charters all over the world. In early 1988, they got a contract to base an airplane in Sicily and they needed another captain right away. Low cost airlines such as Total scrimped with training and relied on the experience of pilots from out-of-business airlines, such as Braniff and Wien. So after a hurried check-out as captain, I was sent to Sigonella on Sicily for a month, and from there I flew to Bahrain, Athens, and Incirlik at Adana, Turkey.

Shortly after departing Incirlik on one flight, I heard some screaming coming from the cabin. A flight attendant got on the intercom and said "There are mice running around all over back here." We did the best that we could to get the situation under control until landing at Athens. Apparently they came aboard in some boxes that were loaded at Incirlik.

I also spent a couple of months on a wet lease from Total Air to Garuda Indonesia Airlines, flying out of Jakarta to places like Hong Kong; Manila; Bali; Madras, India; Abu Dhabi; Riyadh; and Jeddah. When I told Barbara that I was going to have to go to Indonesia and fly out of there for a while, she said, "The kids and I are going too." She convinced the kids' teachers that this would be a great education for my stepdaughter, Suzanne, and stepson, Eric, (Kim, Kurt, and Kent were grown and gone by this time) so they joined me on a trip to Jakarta. As it turned out, I was part of the crew that ferried the airplane to Jakarta so Barbara and the children had the whole airplane of 350 seats to themselves with about ten flight attendants to wait on them.

ON MY FIRST TRIP TO HONG KONG, I had two Garuda Indonesia Airline captains onboard in the jump seats. We had been having trouble with the number one throttle linkage on that airplane since leaving Los Angeles. It would not go all the way to full takeoff power and sometimes it would jam in intermediate positions. We kept writing it up and they kept signing it off as fixed at Jakarta. On this flight, sure enough, I did not quite get full throttle and when I tried to reduce power to climb power, I could not move it back. I had to yank hard on it and it finally let go, causing the airplane to do a big yaw. Everything was fine until the approach to Hong Kong, which was still the original airport at Kowloon that had an exciting approach even on a good day because of a sharp turn that was required over the high part of the city. On this day, the weather was right at minimums making the approach even more interesting. When you reached minimums at Hong Kong, you looked for a big checkerboard red and white panel mounted on the side of a hill. Then you followed a lead-in strobe light over a hill and down the other side to the airport. My co-pilot, Tom Zundel, a former Wien pilot, said, "Keep the wingtip out of the clotheslines."

Again, I could not get the power off on the number one engine without giving it a big yank, which again resulted in a big swerve. I don't think the Garuda captains were very impressed with our operation. Cathay Pacific Airlines was contracted to do our maintenance at Hong Kong and I refused to take the plane until it was definitely fixed. They found the problem in the left wing where some bolts had come loose and jammed a bell crank in the throttle linkage.

The three years with Total Air were the most strenuous flying of my career. I was tired all the time. The airline kept basing us in different cities where we had to pay our own hotel and expenses. We also did not have any jump seat or pass privileges with any other airlines; however, once in a while I was able to talk a captain out of a jump seat.

Eventually the travel agency the airline was associated with went out of business, which seriously affected the revenue. Total Air was then sold to some New York investors and they changed the name to Air America (no connection to the CIA Air America). They started selling off the airplanes and parts, padding their pockets, and continued to operate with leased airplanes until the FAA shut them down in 1990 due to the lack of maintenance. My last flight was from Minneapolis to Las Vegas. When I returned home to Seattle, I found out about the shutdown and so that flight was my last FAR 121 scheduled airline flight. I turned sixty soon after that and retired.

At my retirement party I said that it was probably a good time to retire. It didn't seem to matter anymore how good a pilot I was as much as how fast I could type. Autopilot technology had taken over. I had to admit that while flying the L-1011, I discovered that the autoland capability of that airplane could do a better job landing the airplane in very bad conditions than most pilots could. In a way, I was happy to be done with the commuting and the long flying hours with minimum sleep, but I knew at some point I would have to find some income.

IN THE SUMMERS OF 1990 AND 1991, I filled in for Lowell Thomas Jr. doing sightseeing flights around Mount McKinley. I enjoyed those times because the lodges there had such a spectacular view of the mountain and the service and accommodations were extraordinary. Barbara sometimes came with me and cherishes the time she was able to spend there.

The Soloy 207 was ideal for the McKinley sightseeing flights because it performed well from the small strip and could climb fast to the sightseeing altitude and descend fast without worry of shock cooling the engine. I found that I needed to be very aware of the winds around the mountain to avoid turbulence. I did not like to hear my passengers scream.

One of the things I liked to do for my passengers was to fly straight toward the Wickersham Wall. The wall had a near vertical drop of about 14,000 feet and the magnificence of the wall made it look closer than it really was. I would ask them to tell me when I should start my turn to avoid hitting it and when they said "Now!" I continued to fly a long way before turning. It really showed them how big the mountain was and they were always amazed.

During the days that I could not fly due to the mountain weather, I often pitched in to help the lodge owners build new log cabins for guests. I don't know if I was much help but I did learn how to build log cabins. Other times I would go to the big lodge where there were a lot of books about Alaska to read, many of which were written by people who had climbed McKinley in the past. One day I picked up a book and was well into it when I realized that it was written by the British climbers to whom we had made an airdrop from the Air Rescue SA-16 in 1956 on the Muldrow Glacier. The writer talked about what a thrill it was to see the SA-16 swoop down the glacier and pinpoint the drops right into their camp. I was pleased to see that in writing.

In 1992, while I was visiting Richard in Fairbanks, I learned that Cliff Everts at Everts Air Fuel could use another C-46 pilot during the summer months. I stayed with Richard and his wife, Sally, during my flying there. As a captain, my first co-pilot was Don Hulshizer. Don was a longtime Wien pilot and had been flying captain for Cliff for many years, although by this point he preferred to fly co-pilot. They put us on the scheduling board as the Geritol brothers.

The chief pilot, Ron Clem, re-qualified me and one of my first trips as captain was to Rampart on the Yukon River. I asked Cliff if the runway had been lengthened because the last time I was there forty years prior it was only 2,500 feet. He said no, it was the same length. I guess I had in excess of 3,500 hours in a C-46 at that time but I had never landed one on a 2,500-foot runway.

When I landed at Rampart, I used the technique that I had always used at Wien. Back then, being a scheduled airline, we were limited to 4,000-foot runways in order to conform to accelerated stop distance requirements for takeoff, even with an empty airplane. Everts Air Fuel operated as a cargo carrier under FAR 125 and the accelerated stop requirements did not apply. I just barely got it stopped at Rampart so, for me, that called for a reevaluation of technique on my part. Everts pilots were very competent on these short fields and I figured it out very quickly: slow to 80 knots on short final, land three points near the approach end, and never pull the flaps up after landing.

In July 1992, I was sent to Bethel to make a few trips hauling bulk fuel to Nyac. After making several trips, I was asked to take 2,000 gallons of bulk jet fuel to Kwigillingok (Kwig), a small village south of Bethel. The fuel was for a helicopter that would be doing some kind of survey work in that area.

The C-46 had two 1,000-gallon tanks installed for this purpose. I looked in the Alaska supplement of the airport/facility directory and it showed the length at 2,500 feet and the width as 35 feet. The length did not concern me but I thought the width was a little narrow. I expressed my concern to Fairbanks and the scheduler said in a somewhat irritated voice, "Merrill, if you don't want to do it, we will get someone else." I thought, if someone else could do it, so can I. After all, there would be 7½ feet on either side of the 20-foot tread on the C-46. I was also operating under the assumption that they had landed the C-46 there before.

We loaded up the C-46 with the 2,000-gallon load and my co-pilot did the walk around ahead of time. During the walk around he discovered that some of the bolts that held the tail wheel casting in place were broken and hanging by the safety wire. This obviously weakened the structure and it had to be fixed. We called Fairbanks for the new bolts and they said that the bolts would be on the next MarkAir flight to Bethel.

I was still concerned about the condition of the Kwig runway so I asked a local pilot about it and he said that he would fly me down there in his Cessna 180 so that I could look at it. He said that he first had to make a trip for Arctic Circle Air, the airline he flew for, and then he would take me.

The next day we were waiting in the terminal for our parts to come in and we heard a turboprop airplane taking off. All of a sudden we heard a thump and then silence. Fearing the worst, we ran to the door of the terminal facing the airport and saw wreckage in the form of an unrecognizable pile of aluminum. My co-pilot immediately started running across the ramp to the airplane and just before he got there, the wreckage exploded in a big fireball. He was seconds from being cremated. Someone up above was certainly looking after him but the Skyvan pilots were not so fortunate.

The airplane was an Arctic Circle Air twin engine turboprop Shorts Skyvan and I wondered if the pilot who was going to take me to Kwig had been in it. It turned out that he was not the pilot but he was on the runway in a Cessna 207 in position for takeoff behind the Skyvan and watched the whole disaster.

The investigation later determined that the Skyvan had a load of fuel in fifty-five-gallon barrels destined for Chevak. Normally the barrels would be standing up but for some reason they were lying on their sides, I supposed for the conveniences of loading and unloading, and were not well tied down. The acceleration and initial climb angle broke the restraints and the barrels rolled to the rear of the airplane, causing the airplane to pitch up into an uncontrollable climb until it stalled and crashed. If the barrels had to be placed on their sides, they should have been positioned lengthwise in the cargo compartment so they would not roll back.

Having witnessed the crash from his 207, my 180 pilot was in no condition to be able to take me to Kwig. The parts for my C-46 came in and the bolts were replaced. I decided to go to Kwig without being able to look at it first. When I made a pass over the runway, it looked doable so I set up for the landing. Because of the short runway, the width did not look that narrow. Normally when you get close to touching down on a runway, you expect the runway to get wider in the windshield as you get close to the ground. That did not seem to happen. The runway did not get wider and I touched down close to the approach end and bounced a little because I was not expecting the ground so soon. I favored the left side a little on rollout because the runway was so narrow that I could not see the right edge of the runway from the left seat. When we came to a stop the left wheel was up to the axle in soft gravel. After landing we discovered that of the thirty-five-foot width, only about twenty feet of the middle of the runway was hard enough to support the C-46.

Normally you would expect a wider area at the ends to be able to turn around. I don't know why I did not notice that there was no wide turn-around at the ends. After getting out of the airplane, a little Native boy came up and said, "Wow! Is this a jumbo jet?" In that moment I realized that Kwig had never seen a C-46 before.

I needed to set up and transfer the fuel to the bladder we carried but it was supposed to be placed on a gravel ramp at the midpoint of the runway. There was no way that the airplane could be moved to that point with 14,000 pounds of bulk fuel onboard. We were concerned that without a solid base to put the bladder, there was more likelihood of a fuel leakage. However, I had no choice but to unload the bladder onto the tundra alongside the runway near where we were stuck and unload the fuel there.

I wondered if we were ever going to get the C-46 out of there. I was able to commandeer a grader from the local school and enough cable to attempt to tow the airplane backwards. We also had to acquire enough lumber to build a ramp so we could get the left wheel out of the muck. After a lot of shoveling, we finally got the wheel out of the deep hole and started towing the plane backwards. But we would go a little distance and then the right wheel would get into a soft area and swing the tail to the right, and then the left wheel would sink again, and back and forth. When the tail would swing, the cables would hit the tail wheel doors and I was afraid of ripping them off. I asked my co-pilot to sit in the pilot's seat and pump enough brake pressure and use the brakes to try to keep the tail from swinging from one side to the other while I shouted directions from near the grader. After about four hours of agonizing foot by foot, rearward movement, we got the airplane back to some fairly solid ground at the midpoint in the runway. It appeared we had about a thousand feet of runway ahead of us then and I thought that would be enough for the C-46 to get off with no load and half flap. I said, "That's far enough." I did not want to go farther because that end of the runway looked worse than what we had struggled through already.

My co-pilot came out of the cockpit and said, "Merrill, the runway behind us is not going to do us any good."

I replied, "I don't see a runway behind us. All I see is a muddy road." With half flaps, we were able to make the takeoff with room to spare. Years later I found out the actual dimensions of the runway were 1,840 feet long and 40 feet wide.

A few days after that incident, I was talking to my son Kent about the experience and he told me I must have been mistaken. He said, "You didn't land at Kwig. That's a Twin Otter airport and not big enough for a C-46. You must have it confused with another airport." Kent was very familiar with Kwigillingok because he was flying for Era Aviation in Twin Otters and had flown there many times. Well, I was not mistaken about that mud hole but Kent was hard to convince.

In retrospect, I am the one who made a bad judgment call, not Everts Air Fuel. The captain is always responsible for bad decisions.

IN NOVEMBER 1992, I STARTED FLYING FOR JOE Soloy again, this time doing helicopter flight testing with the installation of the dual pack Allison engine in the Bell Long Ranger helicopter. The conversion was called Gemini. Joe was a hard worker and contributed much to the development of aviation. He also developed a dual pack Pratt and Whitney PT-6 combination driving a five-bladed propeller. The dual pack was first installed in the single engine de Havilland Otter as a test bed only. I made the first flight in the Otter and five days later we were in New Orleans for the annual National Business Aviation Association (NBAA) convention. Joe's plan was to convert the Cessna Caravan with this engine so it would be legal for air taxi operators to carry passengers IFR (meaning, in instrument conditions). It was a great idea but when the FAA later legalized single engine IFR air taxi operations in turbine powered aircraft, this put a damper on future sales of the dual pack. On the way back from the NBAA convention, we stopped at the Cessna and Beech factories in Wichita, Kansas. The Beech engineers were very impressed and talked about using the dual pack on the King Air by removing the wing engines and mounting the dual pack in the nose. On the demonstration flight they asked how it would perform on one engine. I demonstrated by starting only one engine and showing them that the takeoff and climb were comparable to the single engine turbine Otter.

When we got back to Olympia, I continued with the certification testing. One of the tests required going to 30,000 feet to check oil pressure in different bank and climb angles. Being that high in a small airplane is a little unusual and the feeling of height is more pronounced. Later, when I was doing high altitude tests in the Allison dual pack Bell Long Ranger, the feeling of height became a little scary. It is very different from flying in an airplane at that altitude.

My experience doing the flight testing in the Otter got me thinking that the best way to configure a two engine airplane would be with a dual pack that could drive one propeller. Some might say, "What if the gearbox or propeller fail? Then you lose both engines." My response would be that the gearbox developed by the Soloy Corporation was overbuilt to the point that a failure would be very rare as opposed to the accident rate caused by pilot error from mishandling an engine-out procedure, losing an engine at the wrong time, dealing with the reduced performance on one engine with differential thrust, feathering the wrong engine, etc. With a dual pack driving one propeller, the differential thrust is gone. If you lost an engine, there would be nothing to do but fly the airplane. You wouldn't have to worry about feathering an engine and there is no directional minimum control airspeed. When I first flew the DC-3 in 1950, there were fourteen memory items on the engine-out checklist, the last one being feathering the engine. With the dual pack configuration, there would be no immediate actions to accomplish but to just fly the airplane.

For several years I alternated between flying for Soloy, Lowell Thomas Jr., and Everts Air Fuel. In the middle of jumping from job to job, in 1992 I started volunteer flying for the Confederate Air Force, now called the Commemorative Air Force, and that opened up a whole new chapter for me.

15

For the Love of Flying

The B-25s that Merric had operated for firefighting had changed hands several times after we sold them and before BLM stopped using them. Don Gilbertson had two of them that used to belong to Richard and me, and around 1978 I expressed some interest to him in buying one of them. Don was asking $10,000 for one so I needed to think about it. A month or two later, when I was still trying to justify buying it back, I ran into him at Chefs Inn in Anchorage where I was having dinner with my wife and he said, "Hey, Merrill, when are you going to buy my B-25?"

I said, "Oh, Don, right now I would not be able to pay more than $5,000 for it."

He said, "Sold."

I thought, *Oh my gosh. What have I done?* I had to go back to the table and tell my wife that we just bought a bomber.

When I first looked at it I could not turn the props in either direction. That did not look good. I was used to hydraulic locks in the cylinders but I had never experienced a prop not turning backwards or even moving at all. After buying the plane, I towed it over to Merric's hangar and started working on it. I removed all the lower plugs and waited until the oil stopped draining out of the cylinders. After that, when I attempted to move the propeller, I was surprised that it moved freely in either direction. We put some gas and new batteries in it and it started up right away, and the run-up checked out great.

Three years later, I was introduced to the Planes of Fame Museum in Chino, California, by my good friend Joe Haley, who flew for Wien Air Alaska beginning in the early '70s. He suggested I donate the B-25 to the museum, which I did. I was then able to fly some great warbirds at the museum, including the Douglas A-26, North American P-51, the Japanese Zero, and the B-25. I believe my old B-25 is now based in the Palm Springs Museum.

BY 1980, I HAD BEEN SAVING MONEY FOR years to be able to buy a P-51. But every time I got enough saved, the going rate went out of reach again. I suggested to my brother, Richard, that we go in together on one. He suggested we get one with two engines, a P-38, because at that time they were selling for less than a P-51. I thought that was a good idea. We found one in Okmulgee, Oklahoma, that had been sitting for four years. In Oklahoma, I made arrangements for the fellow who had been flying it for the previous owner to ferry it for us to Tulsa for relicensing. In the meantime, I applied for a letter of authorization (LOA) from the FAA. After I received it, the fellow who was going to ferry the plane to Tulsa said, "Why don't you fly it since you now have an LOA?"

Why not? I thought.

My friend Joe Haley came to Okmulgee to help get it ready to fly. The first time I taxied it, I applied the brakes to keep the speed down and the pedals went all the way to the bottom. There were no brakes. I madly started pumping the brakes and finally they locked up. I shut down the engines and called the original pilot. I explained what happened and he said, "Yep, that's the way they work."

The mechanics had already explained to me that the brake system had been modified to be able to use system pressure for better braking but they had failed to explain how to use them. You had to work the pedals up and down carefully until enough volume of hydraulic fluid got to the brakes. You were not supposed to release the brakes; otherwise you had to start all over. I found that metering the brake pressure was very difficult, but I eventually got the hang of it. It was a bad modification.

I went ahead and prepared to ferry the plane to Tulsa. The runway was a little short at Okmulgee so there was not much time to check things out on the roll. About the time that I got to the point where I would not be able to stop, the left engine started backfiring. I pulled the power way back and it smoothed out. I definitely did not want any problems on my first flight in a P-38. I was required to leave the gear down because the plane was being flown on a ferry permit and because no jacks were available at Okmulgee to raise the airplane up for the retraction test.

As I leveled out at 3,000 feet, my heart was finally starting to settle down. All of a sudden, the right engine quit cold, just as if I had turned the ignition switch off. All the engine instruments looked normal and I tried everything I could think of to get it to run. Even though I increased power on the left engine, I was still descending. I feathered the right engine and it seemed like it was a long time before it stopped windmilling. The plane became much easier to control after the prop feathered but I was still descending slightly, so I raised the gear.

Another fine fix I got myself into. Joe Haley and two mechanics were flying alongside of me in a Bonanza and they were surprised to see the right propeller stop and the gear come up. I was not able to talk to them and, in fact, I was not able to raise Tulsa tower either. The radio I had was an old World War II–type dynamotor powered radio and the frequencies were badly out of calibration. I finally got the tower on ground frequency and advised them of my situation. I felt a lot better once I was over the field. At that point all I had to worry about was whether the gear would come down and lock. I set up for an overhead approach and lowered the gear. When the green lights did not immediately come down I began to think the worst.

Finally, three green lights appeared. The landing worked out fine and I thought I was going to make it all the way to the hangar on one engine with a fast taxi until the tower told me to hold at an intersection of a parallel runway for an aircraft on final. I knew that the plane's tow bar was still in Okmulgee so this might be a big problem. I could not taxi right off since I did not have nose wheel steering. I struggled with it and finally got it to move straight by using the left brake heavily. When I arrived at the ramp the brake was smoking.

When the carburetors went in for overhaul, they found that the problem with the right engine was that the diaphragms in the carburetor had dried up from sitting in the hot sun for four years without fuel and they had ruptured. This shut off all the fuel to the engine, even though fuel pressure showed as "normal." I am so thankful that the other carburetor did not fail. I went back home while the carburetors were being overhauled.

When I came back a few weeks later after the overhauled carburetors had been reinstalled and after the plane had been relicensed, I took off for Chino. I got only about twenty minutes out when the left oil cooler shutter went full-closed in the automatic position and the oil temperature went to red line, so I had to put the cooler doors in the full-open position. There was no manual intermediate positioning, only full-open, full-closed, and automatic. In the full-open position it would cause the airplane to buffet and the oil temperature would get too cold. I thought that I was going to have to open and close the cooler doors all the way to Chino. Pretty soon the right engine started to backfire and had to be run at well below cruise power to keep it running. Things were starting to pile up so I turned around and went back to Tulsa International.

After I landed, legendary P-38 pilot Lefty Gardner walked up to the airplane and yelled up to me, "You have a coolant leak coming out of the left engine." Good thing I turned around. A hose clamp was rubbing on the aluminum coolant tube and had worn a hole in it. I would not have been able to keep that engine running for long.

I had the repairs made and after I completed a local test flight, Lefty jumped up on the wing and said, "Merrill, don't ever sell this airplane. It is going to be worth a lot of money someday. It is a famous World War II fighter and there are only five of them still flying."

The next time, I had better luck departing Tulsa but not too far out of Chino the left propeller stuck in the fixed pitch position. After landing at Chino, we found the problem in the cannon plug to the prop governor on the Curtiss Electric prop.

On a local flight at Chino, I gave Joe Haley a ride. This airplane had been modified for a 2-place cockpit because at one time it had been used for high altitude mapping. During my flight with Joe, a lot of smoke appeared in the cockpit. I called the tower, informed them about the smoke, and they cleared me to land and scrambled the fire trucks. I then turned off the electrical power and landed. That problem turned out to be a resistor in the high boost pump electrical wiring, which had started to smoke when I turned the boost pump on for landing.

This airplane was starting to wear me down. It seemed that I had some kind of an emergency every time I flew it. With the help of Steve Hinton and his crew at Fighter Rebuilders in Chino, eventually we were able to get the bugs worked out. We kept the plane based in Chino and flew it a few times, including at one of the big annual air shows sponsored by the Planes of Fame. Richard and I planned to eventually fly it to Seattle but after about a year we decided to sell it to Charles Nichols at the Yanks Air Museum in Chino.

Richard and I regret that we did not take Lefty Gardner's advice and keep the airplane. I am sure we would have figured out a way to keep it if we had known that about a year and a half later, one would sell for $1.5 million at an auction in California. We paid about $190,000 and sold it for the same after throwing a lot of money at it.

A FEW YEARS LATER, I BOUGHT ANOTHER B-25 that had been sitting in the airplane graveyard at Fairbanks for about fifteen years. It had been used as a fire fighter and was also used to dump coal dust on the Tanana River in the spring to expedite the melting of the river ice. This reduced the danger of flooding during breakup. I paid more for that B-25 than I had for the first one and I had to do a lot more work to get it ferryable. Jim Anderson, a long-time friend of mine and a mechanic, helped me change several cylinders, and Jeff Thomas, a Wien Airlines pilot, helped me get it ready to ferry to Chino for restoration at Aero Trader. After getting it to Seattle, we parked it there until the following summer. During a test flight in the spring in preparation for the continuation to Chino, the right engine quit on final to landing. The problem turned out to be a ruptured diaphragm in the carburetor, just like what had happened to me during my first flight in the P-38. Carburetors do not like years of storage without fuel in them.

I sold the B-25 to Stephen Grey in England around 1990, just before it was fully restored, and it remained in England for several years. It was recently purchased by John Sessions for his Heritage Flight Foundation Museum at Paine Field, Washington, and is now named *Grumpy*.

I WAS NOT ONLY INTERESTED IN OWNING MY own vintage planes, but I enjoyed any opportunity to fly them as well. In 1993 my neighbor at the air-field neighborhood in Kent, Denny Newell, called me one day and said that he had talked to Russ Drosendahl, a member of the Southern California

Wing of the Confederate Air Force (CAF). The wing was based at Camarillo, California, and they operated a Curtiss C-46 named *China Doll*. They were having a hard time finding experienced C-46 pilots and he told Russ about me. Denny suggested that I call Russ, operations officer of the C-46 wing, and when I did he said that he sure would like to talk to me. I got on a flight and went to Camarillo. I then joined the CAF and soon found myself their C-46 chief pilot. Since the Seattle FAA flight standards district office had designated me as a C-46 examiner, I started doing quite a bit of training and type rating check rides in the squadron.

The first time that I flew the C-46 to the big annual CAF Air Show in Midland, Texas, the CAF was also operating another C-46 called *Tinker Belle*. Their pilot was due for an annual check ride. Vern Thorpe was the CAF chief transport pilot and would normally administer this flight check but he was temporarily unable to fly due to a health problem. When he found out that I was an FAA C-46 designee, he asked me to do the check ride. I told him I could do the check to satisfy the FAA but that I was not a CAF designated check pilot. He said, "I can fix that."

He went to his longtime friend and CAF's chief bomber check pilot, Randy Sohn, and asked him to give me a check ride so I could be listed as a CAF check pilot. Randy was not happy because he was getting ready to go back home to Minnesota and had to change his plans. I could tell he was upset. I did not know anything about Randy and he did not know anything about me. When we were getting ready to start engines, with Randy in the left seat, I asked him if he had any tail wheel time. He said, "Yes." We taxied out and took off. He said he had never flown a C-46 before but I was impressed by how well he handled the airplane. Everything was going fine when he said that he wanted to do some single engine work. We simulated a shutdown and he set up to do a single engine landing. He asked for full flaps a little early, I thought, and then he descended too soon, to the point that I had to take over and bring the other engine back to life and reduce flaps. I was surprised he did this so I kept a real close eye on him. After landing he started to run the airplane off the taxi way. I jumped on the brakes and yelled, "I got it!" I finally figured out that I was being tested. Well, I should have realized that that was what the flight was all about anyway.

Apparently Randy was satisfied that I was qualified to be a check pilot. That was the beginning of a long friendship. I later found out that, indeed,

Randy had some tail wheel time. He was one of the most experienced war-bird pilots in the nation as well as a senior Northwest Airlines captain.

I learned much from Randy and he opened doors for me to be able to fly more CAF airplanes, such as the B-29 and the B-24. In time he was selected to put together a group of examiners to be authorized by the FAA to administer check rides for type ratings and recurrent check rides in dozens of vintage transports, airliners, and bombers. This group was to be called National Designated Pilot Examiner Resource (NDPER) and was initiated because the FAA was losing qualified World War II examiners experienced in vintage bombers and transports. A search began to find airmen with multiple type ratings in these kinds of aircraft. It was a combined effort by the FAA, the Experimental Aircraft Association (EAA), and the Aircraft Owners and Pilots Association (AOPA). Randy asked me if I would participate. Initially there were only about five of us but I don't think there were ever more than ten, at least while I was active.

I lasted a few years in that role but I eventually resigned. I started out being able to do the check ride in the right seat but soon the FAA required us to sit in the jump seat on check rides if we had not had an annual recurrent check ride in the airplane within the last twelve months. The right seat needed to have a current pilot but it could be just a co-pilot with second in command currency. After having to fly out of the jump seat a few times to save the airplane, I decided this situation was not good for my longevity.

Several aspiring C-46 pilots joined the Southern California Wing in hopes of qualifying in the C-46. One said he had 3,000 hours in a C-46 but that it had been about thirty years since he had last flown one. When I flew with him it was hard to tell that he had ever flown a C-46. This is the way it was going until one day Randy Sohn called and put me in touch with John Deakin as a possible candidate. John said he had about 1,500 hours in the C-46 with the CIA (Air America) but he said it was a long time ago. At that time he was a 747 captain. I did not expect much but when I flew with him, I was delighted. He flew it like he had been flying it every day. John went on to become a big help with training and proficiency. The C-46 is an airplane that requires more training than airplanes like the DC-3 because the rudder is not effective on takeoff until about 50 knots and, with the large fuselage, it is harder to handle in a crosswind. The use of full aileron control and differential power has to be learned for maximum advantage.

The wing was interested in acquiring a B-25 and since I was fresh out of B-25s to donate, they bid on a B-25 that headquarters had acquired. While I was helping to get that plane into shape in Midland, I connected with Tom Cloyd, who was the CAF squadron commander of the B-29/B-24 squadron. He was looking for pilots with four engine experience and when I told him about mine, in the DC-4 and Constellation, he asked me to join them on tour. I did a brief stint with him then but I didn't fly the B-29, known as *FIFI*, again until the next year, 1994, when I got a call from the squadron operations officer, Dale Markgraf, saying that they could sure use me.

I joined up again with Tom Cloyd in Jacksonville and he let me fly left seat to Savannah, Georgia. We did a press flight in Savannah and then Tom announced that we that we were going to do my check ride for my letter of authorization (LOA) in the B-29. I was very honored to have Bob Robbins onboard as an extra crew member for my checkout. In 1943, Bob had taken over the initial flight testing of the number one B-29 after Eddie Allen was killed in the number two airplane, and Bob had also been the first pilot to fly the B-47. Bob liked to tour with *FIFI* when it came through Florida, where he lived, and would give many cockpit tours. I learned a lot about the B-29 from Bob. He was among the most humble men I have ever met.

After the flight, I was surprised to hear Tom say that I was now a B-29 pilot and I was on my own. He was going home. I stayed with *FIFI* for the next five weeks, touring from Savannah, Georgia, to Knoxville, Tennessee, and Lexington, Kentucky, to Cincinnati and Cleveland, Ohio, and finally to Grand Rapids, Michigan, where I was then relieved.

At Lexington we encountered what was either a big twister or a small tornado. As the wind picked up, I made a dash for the B-29 bomb bay and crawled up inside. The rain was blowing horizontally and it was the only place to stay dry. I thought I felt the airplane start to move and I realized that this would not be a good place to be if the B-29 blew away. The wind was gone in about a minute. As I climbed back out of the bomb bay I noticed that the propeller blades had rotated to a different position. We always positioned the props after shutdown so that the blades were vertical and horizontal. I also noticed that the C-46, *Tinker Belle*, was in a different place and that quite a bit of damage was done to the elevator. The wind had picked it up and set it on top of some parked cars. The B-24 was also damaged when the C-46 hit it and repairs had to be made to the wingtip.

During the next few weeks, I was also trained and checked out in the B-24, *Diamond Lil*. Over the next several years I flew tours in the B-29 and the B-24.

I was privileged to fly *FIFI* to the 1995 annual Oshkosh air show. Let me tell you, if you are going to fly an airplane to Oshkosh, do it in a B-29, or maybe the SST. The controllers virtually cleared the airspace to give us priority for landing. I flew to Oshkosh a year or so later in my Grumman Widgeon and there was no such priority. Randy was pilot in command but he seemed to always let me have the glory and gave me the left seat. That was the year that EAA had planned a massive flyover celebrating the fiftieth anniversary of the end of World War II. I think there were 175 World War II–era fighters, bombers, transports, and trainers participating that year. During the air show, I was privileged to fly the B-24 and Randy flew *FIFI*. A lot of planning went into the choreography and timing for the different types to make their flybys. The national anthem was played all over the airfield and it was piped up to all the aircraft. It was a very emotional experience and we were informed after landing that there was not a dry eye anywhere in the crowd.

During the annual CAF air show in September 1995, we had a tragic accident. The CAF had recently finished a long restoration of a very rare Martin B-26. Vern Thorp and Randy Sohn had completed the test flights the day before and that day Vern took five British enthusiasts on a local flight. Tom Cloyd had become very interested in the B-26 and was hoping to get checked out in it. He made arrangements to go along on this flight.

I was in the process of administering a check ride and I was in the maintenance library conducting an oral on the B-25 when we were interrupted by the crew chief for *FIFI*, Don Davis, to tell us that the B-26 just went in. We were stunned. I remembered seeing Tom walking around the B-26 before the flight so I assumed that he was onboard. There were no survivors and I don't think they ever figured out what happened. It was a terrible loss. Tom's wife, Margaret, was an active supporter in the squadron and she was there when it happened. Margaret continued to be active in the squadron for many years, primarily responsible for the PX sales on tour. The B-29/B-24 squadron was Tom and Margaret's family.

THE HERITAGE FLIGHT MUSEUM WAS FOUNDED BY RETIRED Major General William Anders, on Orcas Island, in the San Juan Islands in Washington

State. It is now located at Skagit Regional (Bayview) Airport, Washington, and has an impressive display of World War II airplanes. Barbara and I had moved to the island in 1995 to enjoy our retirement years. Eventually we came in contact with the Anders family, which resulted in many more happy years in aviation. Bill asked me to become involved with the museum as its Director of Flight Safety, which entailed flying several of the museum airplanes and meeting some very interesting people.

Bill had recently retired as CEO of General Dynamics, following a very impressive career. His bio alone would be longer than this book. Since he was one of the crew of Apollo 8, the first flight to the moon, with Frank Borman and Jim Lovell, he entertained some very interesting NASA guests, most of whom I had the privilege of meeting.

Bill likes to keep conversations on the lighter side and loves to banter with friends. One of the stories Bill likes to tell about me happened when the legendary Wally Schirra paid him a visit. Wally was the only astronaut to have flown in the Mercury, Gemini, and Apollo programs. Bill introduces everyone as the "world's second greatest pilot." I tell the person that we are still trying to figure out who the greatest pilot is.

When Wally saw my beautifully restored Grumman Widgeon amphibian sitting on the museum ramp, he was very impressed. I asked him if he would like to fly it. He said he sure would. As we were taxiing out, Bill's son Alan was taxiing in and asked us where we were going. I said we were going to Lake Whatcom, and he asked if he could go with us. As it turned out, we were sure glad to have him onboard.

It was an unusually warm day and as we continued to do some landings and takeoffs, the oil temperatures started to go over the red line. I said that we should land and let the temperatures cool off. After the oil temperatures died down I attempted to start the engines. The right engine started right away but the left engine would not start. It turned out that the heat from the engine rose to the top of the engine, cooking the magnetos. The last overhaul of the magnetos did not oven check the condensers to make sure the coils were still functional in hot temperatures. All we could do was taxi in circles. I thought, *Oh well, we can just paddle to shore and wait till the mags cool.* But the only problem was that I did not have a paddle onboard, which we probably could have used as a rudder to steer the plane to dry land. Finally, Alan said he would jump in and tow the

Widgeon. He stripped down and tied a rope to the nose, put it in his teeth, and got us to shore.

Well, at least I did have a rope onboard. Fortunately, Wally really enjoyed the adventure and found it very humorous. Alan, on the other hand, I'm not so sure about.

A few days later, I was asked to take Bill somewhere in the Widgeon and when Wally got in, he sat in the co-pilot's seat. I said to Wally, "I think the general might like to sit there." He said, "A Navy lieutenant commander is a higher rank than an Air Force general." So Bill sat in the back. I thought that I had removed the cover for the pitot tube, the probe that registers airspeed. As we started our takeoff roll, I noticed that the airspeed indicator did not show any airspeed indication. I was hoping that no one would notice but Bill sure did and was delighted to come forward to tap Wally on the shoulder and point to the covered airspeed probe. I don't think I'd ever forgotten the cover before so why did it have to be at a time like this. My response to Bill and Wally was that I usually keep it covered because I am a "seat of the pants" bush pilot and the airspeed indicator can be a distraction. I am not sure they bought that. I look forward to any time I can tattle on Bill.

When Bill was collecting airplanes for the museum, he asked me to accompany him to Fort Worth to take delivery of a Boeing Stearman. On the way back to Ramona, California, we spent the night with his mission commander, Frank Borman of Apollo 8 and his wife, Susan, in Santa Teresa, New Mexico. I wish I had recorded the conversations about the early astronaut days.

Bill has two fine sons, Alan and Greg, who are excellent formation pilots (as is Bill) and will continue to be a resource for the museum.

ONE DAY IN 1998, WHILE FLYING *FIFI* AT the annual CAF air show at Midland, I was told that we were going to do a VIP flight. As I walked out to the B-29, I thought I recognized Paul Tibbets signing the manifest. Sure enough, it was the one and only Paul Tibbets, who had flown B-17s in Europe and later flew many missions in the B-29 over Japan. He was the pilot of the *Enola Gay*, which, of course, dropped the first atomic bomb on Hiroshima. What a great honor to meet him, let alone to have him onboard a flight in the B-29.

I had heard that General Tibbits was no longer willing to fly in *FIFI*. I said, "General, are you going to fly with us today?"

He said, "Yes, Mary Alice wanted to ride in *FIFI* and insisted that I go along." Mary Alice was a close friend of the general's. Also onboard was Paul Tibbits IV, the general's grandson, who was a B-2 pilot and Commander G. Newhouse, the commander of all the F-18 squadrons east of the Mississippi. I made a copy of the manifest and it hangs on my wall.

When it was time for the flight with General Tibbets to return to Midland we were told that the airport was closed for another hour because the Blue Angels were practicing for the next day's air show. This was a big disappointment because the B-29 was burning about 400 gallons of fuel an hour and the squadron was struggling for financial survival. At that time the only revenue that the squadron was able to generate was from cockpit tours at five dollars a head and from PX sales. The cost of engine overhauls was increasing every year because we were losing expertise in the overhaul facilities. Engine overhauls at that time were about $50,000. Now the over-haul costs are probably closer to $100,000 and hourly costs in the air are about $10,000. Fortunately the FAA has now authorized the carrying of paying passengers, which generates much more than five dollars a head for cockpit tours.

Since we had time to kill on our flight, I put General Tibbets in the left seat and his grandson in the right seat for some photos. At one point he said, "Merrill, what do you think our gross weight is now?" I asked our engineer, Mike Looney, to give us a reading on our weight. When I relayed the weight to the general, he said, relying on memory, "I think we can save some fuel if you set the power to such and such manifold pressure and rpm." Sure enough, we were able to remain airborne and saved some fuel. What a memory.

I later encouraged the squadron to install chip detectors in the engines and pre-oilers for the lubrication to start the engines. I think that I had two test flights with newly overhauled engines at Midland where the chip light came on shortly after takeoff, requiring pulling the engine and doing another costly repair, though the repairs were probably less costly because we had the chip detectors. It is a constant struggle to keep *FIFI* flying and although the CAF has managed to convert the engines to a more reliable Curtiss Wright R-3350 and the engines are far more reliable, it is probably a matter of time before it will just be a static display. Come fly with *FIFI* before it is too late.

I FLEW MY LAST TOUR IN *FIFI* IN 2001. My sons, Kurt and Kent, both American Airlines captains, had always felt bad that I did not receive the usual ceremonial fire truck water display over the airplane on my last flight as an airline pilot. I was flying the B-29 on the West Coast tour that year, so Kurt and Kent made arrangements to have the fire trucks at Paine Field in Everett, Washington, provide that service as a surprise. My wife, Barbara, came to Salem, Oregon, to be onboard and to make sure that I would be in the left seat arriving at Paine. I was planning to be in the right seat because I wanted to give some experience to John Deakin, a prospective pilot in command candidate. I told her that this was not her decision. I thought that she wanted me in the left seat if she was going to be onboard.

When it looked like I was going to be stubborn about it, she went to John and explained what the plan was. Then John came to me and said that he thought that he needed more right seat experience before flying from the left seat. Unfortunately, we had some engine trouble and when it looked like we were going to have to cancel the flight for the day, Barbara went ahead on a commercial flight to Seattle. At the last moment, we found the problem to be shorted P leads in the ignition switch and we were able to make it to Paine just before dark.

We usually arrived at new locations on Mondays and then did a press flight. Since it was too late to do a press flight, it was rescheduled for Tuesday morning. Barbara and my two boys were there and Barbara flew with me in the B-29. As we were taxiing in, I was surprised to see the two fire trucks, one on each side. All of a sudden water was everywhere. We had the windows open in the cockpit and we made a mad scramble to get them shut. The fire truck drivers got a big kick out of it.

It was a nice surprise but I was not aware I was planning on retiring from flying the B-29. My family explained that it was a belated gesture for airline retirement. Actually, I flew *FIFI* on only one more leg, Paine to Spokane, and then did some more local training in Spokane. I was scheduled to fly *FIFI* to Alaska the next summer but corrosion was found in the wing during winter overhaul and it did not fly that summer.

I HAVE TO SAY THAT THE PEOPLE I met in the CAF are some of the finest people that I have ever known. They volunteered their time to help keep our history of the fight for freedom alive—such an important lesson for young people today. And several of the crew members with whom I was privileged to fly in *FIFI* were themselves World War II crew members in the B-29: Bob Freeman, J. B. Hudson, Blackie Blackburn, Bob Robbins, Jack Bradshaw. Most of them are gone now but what an honor to have known them and what an honor to have had the opportunity to fly such a valuable and famous airplane. In fact, it is an honor to have known so many of the pilots I have flown with over the years. There just seems to be some kind of commonality that attracts pilots to one another that forms a foundation for long-lasting relationships.

Epilogue

Given that I got bit by the aviation bug early in life, I suppose it is no surprise that I've passed this on to the next generation. I couldn't wait to get my hands on the controls at an early age, and my sons were no different. By the time he was twelve, Kent was doing landings and takeoffs in a Citabria on skis. Before that, at age thirteen, my oldest son, Kurt, hounded me to let him fly our Cessna 185 on floats. I caved in and decided to let him see if he could make the takeoff.

As my dad had done with me in the J-3 Cub, I just sat there next to him and thought he was in for a surprise. I guess I hadn't realized that Kurt had been watching every move I made whenever he flew with me. I sure was paying attention at his age so I don't know why I didn't think that he might also have been paying attention. Anyway, after getting him set up in the pilot's seat with enough cushions, we gave it a go. He put down half flap, advanced the power, pulled back on the elevator, and then let the nose down when we were on the step. When the airplane left the water, he re-trimmed and pulled the throttle back and reduced rpm. As speed picked up he raised the flaps and re-trimmed. It wasn't precise but it was more than I expected from a kid with no training. I was dumbfounded.

As my children began expressing an interest in flying, I soon understood that the perspective of a parent can involve a bit more worrying. When Kurt got hang gliding fever at age twelve, that was the beginning of my gray hairs. Then he graduated to ultralights and the gray hairs kept showing up.

Of course, all this got Kent's attention. We lived on a lake in the Anchorage area and it was a great place for ski planes in the winter and floatplanes in the summer. Kent kept hounding me to let him fly Kurt's Eagle XL ultralight. What a ridiculous idea; he was only thirteen at the time. I finally agreed but I emphasized that he was authorized only to just lift the contraption off the ice and not to gain any altitude. He assured me that he would abide by that limitation. Kent was an outstanding radio control model flyer so I knew he knew something about aerodynamics. He had also been flying my Cessna quite a bit while airborne so I felt confident that everything would work out.

After Kent was strapped in, he pushed the throttle forward. Right away I thought, *OK, it's time for him to pull the throttle back so he won't get too high.* The power did not come back. Instead he began climbing rapidly, and kept climbing. Well, I now knew how it felt to think I had just killed my son.

Kurt tried to calm me down. I was glad to see that Kent stopped climbing and started to come down. He made a nice landing and taxied to where we were standing. As I started in on my tirade, he interrupted and said that Kurt had checked him out in it some time ago. He just needed my retroactive approval. Apparently Kurt had instructed him to not screw around close to the ground. "Get some altitude," he told Kent. "It's much safer." Kurt had been trained by the ultralight guru in the Anchorage area, Mike Jacober, so I guess Kent received some good advice. Both Kurt and Kent are now captains for American Airlines.

My daughter, Kim, got the flying bug also and, at age twenty-one, as soon as she could legally be a flight attendant, she was hired at Wien. In quite a proud moment for me, we were able to crew the inaugural flight from Fairbanks to Seattle together. After Wien shut down, Kim went to work as a flight attendant for Alaska Airlines and figures she'll still be at it into her seventies.

On the seventy-fifth anniversary of the first flight between Anchorage and Fairbanks, made by Noel Wien, in July 1924, Richard and I get ready to reenact our father's historic accomplishment. *Photo © by Myron Wright.*

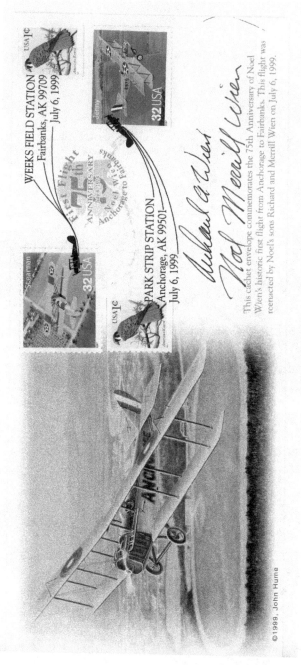

This is the envelope that the Anchorage Post Office printed to be sold at the temporary post office on the Park Strip in commemoration of the seventy-fifth anniversary flight.

IN 1998, RICHARD SAID THAT HE WOULD LIKE to see us do some kind of anniversary flight between Anchorage and Fairbanks to honor our father's flight in July of 1924, the first airplane flight between the two cities. Since we could not duplicate the type of airplane my father flew, a Hisso-powered Standard J-1, Richard said that he would buy a Boeing Stearman, which was at least a biplane. Richard found a nice one in Idaho and I went to look at it. The plane looked great so it was purchased and I flew it to Orcas Island in the San Juans, where Barbara and I were living at the time. I had a nice hangar there so it was a good place to store it until Richard could come get it.

In April 1999, Richard and his son Michael came and flew it up to Fairbanks and Richard's good friend Martin Hale escorted them with his Cessna 180, carrying fuel, baggage, and extra equipment. It was still very cold on the northern part of the route and Richard found out what the early pioneer bush pilots faced flying open cockpit airplanes in Alaska in the 1920s. Martin did not help Richard's spirits much when he said that he had to take off his jacket because it was getting too warm in the Cessna. When Richard and Michael arrived in Fairbanks, they were so stiff from the cold that it took a long time for them to be able to move their limbs enough to exit the airplane.

The idea started out just being a family affair but when the word got around about the upcoming flight, it captured a lot of interest. Ted Spencer, curator at the Alaska Aviation Museum in Anchorage, said, "Richard, why don't you do the departure from the Park Strip in Anchorage?" The Park Strip is the exact location where the first airport was built in 1923, which was on the edge of town back then but is now in downtown Anchorage. Richard didn't think there was much chance of being allowed to take off from the middle of the city but when the mayor of Anchorage heard about the idea, he said, "Let's make it happen." The governor of Alaska said the same thing.

We figured the FAA would certainly not approve it but when the head of the FAA in Alaska heard about it, he too said, "Let's make it happen." That initiated some meetings and planning sessions. Richard asked me to come to Anchorage and confirm that there would be enough room to land and take off there. It looked like it would be possible if a fence was removed, a ditch filled in, a flagpole taken down, and orange marker balls hung from the power lines. When the day came, I made the landing from the front seat to better see the power lines we had to land over. We were amazed at the attention and the effort that took place to make it happen.

There was a big crowd to see us off in Anchorage. When it came time to depart, the head FAA representative came over and requested that Richard make a flyby after the takeoff. Richard asked how low he should make the pass. The FAA fellow said, "As low as you want." Richard came back around and made the pass about 100 feet off the ground, which provided a larger audience to witness. It was a rare sight for the people of Anchorage to see an airplane flying that low over the middle of the city.

When we arrived at Fairbanks there was a strong crosswind so Richard suggested that I make the landing. Knowing that we had a large audience, I didn't want to be responsible for a bad landing, and I knew that Richard could do as well as I could or better, so I refused. He did a great job.

As we pulled up to the ramp in Fairbanks, there was a huge reception there as well, with a big band and speeches. It was nice to discover that people were still very interested in local history and that they felt it was important to commemorate such occasions. My son Kurt bought the Stearman and when he flew it back to New Hampshire where he lived, he and his good friend Tim Knutson, who lived in Wisconsin, stopped off in Cook, Minnesota, where Kurt's grandfather was raised. Many people there still knew the history of Noel Wien and the Wien family. Kurt became a temporary celebrity and it is an experience he will never forget. Dropping in with a biplane on the little town where the family vocation started over eighty years earlier meant that our saga had come full circle. While his arrival was mentioned in the local paper, the significance was even more special among the family.

Without the advancements from the Wright brothers, the industry that provided a living for my father and the two generations that followed wouldn't have been possible, or at least delayed a decade or two and I am grateful for their accomplishments. For this reason, I'm especially proud that the original pilot's license of my father was signed by Orville Wright.

A photo of my daughter, Kimberlee, a flight attendant for Alaska Airlines, her husband Terry, standing behind her, and my sons Kurt and Kent, both of whom fly for American Airlines.

Acknowledgments

The main reason for getting started on this book is I caved in to the many requests that I have received from my children and others.

I want to thank my three children, Kimberlee, Kurt, and Kent and my wife, Barbara, and my stepchildren, Eric Guina and Suzanne Sagiao, for the encouragement and enthusiasm that they showed for the book.

Kristelle and Kerry Sim gave me the final push by offering to help. Their help was interrupted by Kerry's death. My brother, Richard, helped me remember some dates and events that I had forgotten since we shared so many adventures together.

I have been privileged to know some outstanding pilots but my father—Noel Wien—along with Herm Joslyn; Sam White; my brother, Richard; Dick King; and Holger "Jorgy" Jorgensen stand out, not just because of their flying ability, but because of their character and the influence they had on me. There are many more pilots who had a big influence on me but if I tried to name them, I surely would be leaving some out. During the 1940s, Herm was probably the most loyal pilot that Wien Airlines ever had and when I flew for Pan American in 1951, he was like a father to me.

I would also like to thank Lowell Thomas Jr.'s daughter, Anne, for putting me in touch with my publisher, Graphics Arts Books, who have made this endeavor a pleasant experience. Also, my editor, Janet Kimball, has done an amazing job of making my writings more readable.

Further Reading

Doolittle, General Jimmy. *I Could Never Be So Lucky Again*. Atglen, PA: Schiffer Publishing, Ltd., 1994.

Griese, Arnold. *Bush Pilot: Early Alaska Aviator Harold Gillam Sr., Lucky or Legend?* Anchorage: Publication Consultants, 2005.

Harkey, Ira. *Noel Wien: Alaska Pioneer Bush Pilot*. Fairbanks: University of Alaska Press, 1999.

MacLean, Robert Merrill. *Flying Cold: The Adventures of Russel Merrill, Pioneer Alaskan Aviator*. Kenmore, WA: Epicenter Press, 1994.

Page, Dorothy G. *Polar Pilot: The Carl Ben Eielson Story*. Apple Valley, MN: Hobar Publications, 1992.

Potter, Jean. *The Flying North*. Sausalito, CA: Comstock Publishing, 1972.

Rearden, Jim. *Alaska's First Bush Pilots, 1923-30 and the Winter Search in Siberia for Eielson and Borland*. Missoula, MT: Pictorial Histories Publishing Company, Inc., 2009.

_____. *Sam O. White: Tales of a Legendary Wildlife Agent and Bush Pilot*. Missoula, MT: Pictorial Histories Publishing Company, Inc., 2006.

Tordoff, Dirk. *Mercy Pilot: The Joe Crosson Story*. Kenmore, WA: Epicenter Press, 2002.

Aircraft Flown
by Noel Merrill Wien

1. Luscombe
2. T-Craft
3. Aeronca Champ
4. Aeronca Chief
5. Aeronca Sedan (floats)
6. Bellanca Scout
7. Citabria 7ECA
8. Bellanca Skyrocket (floats)
9. Fairchild 24 wheels and floats
10. Fairchild PT-26
11. Fairchild PT-19
12. Fairchild F-27
13. Boeing PT-13
14. Boeing PT-17
15. Boeing 737
16. Boeing 727
17. Boeing B-17
18. Boeing B-29
19. Consolidated LB-30 (B-24)
20. Ryan PT-22
21. Piper J-3
22. Piper PA-11
23. Piper PA-18
24. Piper Pacer
25. Piper Super Cruiser PA12
26. Piper Comanche
27. Piper Apache
28. Piper Seneca
29. Aviat Husky
30. Commonwealth Skyranger
31. Mooney Mite
32. Mooney M-20
33. Fleet 16B
34. Cessna 140 wheels skis and floats
35. Cessna 150
36. Cessna 170 wheels skis and floats
37. Cessna 172
38. Cessna 180 wheels skis and floats
39. Cessna 182
40. Cessna 185 wheels skis and floats
41. Cessna 185 Soloy turbine (floats)
42. Cessna 195 wheels skis and floats
43. Cessna 337 Skymaster
44. Cessna 206 wheels and floats
45. Cessna 206 Soloy Turbine wheels and floats
46. Cessna 207 wheels
47. Cessna 207 Soloy turbine wheels and floats
48. Cessna 208 Soloy PT-6 Dual Pack Turbines
49. Cessna L-19 Bird Dog
50. Republic Seabee
51. Twin Seabee

52	Ranger Grumman Widgeon	87	Consolidated Vultee L-13
53	Super Widgeon	88	Aircoupe
54	Grumman Goose	89	Noorduyn Norseman
55	Grumman Albatross	90	Max Holste Broussard
56	Grumman TBM	91	Fairchild Pilgram
57	Varga 2180 TG	92	Piaggio Royal Gull
58	Stinson L-5	93	Globe Swift
59	Stinson AT-19	94	DHC-2 Beaver wheels and floats
60	Stinson SM8A	95	DHC-3 Otter Soloy Dual
61	Stinson 108		Pack Turbine
62	Beech Bonanza	96	Short Skyvan
63	Beech Baron B-55	97	DH Twin Otter DHC-6
64	North American Navion	98	Fairchild C-82
65	Beech Travel Air B-95	99	Fairchild C-119
66	Beech Twin Bonanza C-50	100	Fairchild C-123
67	Beech Baron 58TC	101	Lockheed T-33
68	Twin Beech C-45	102	Lockheed P-38
69	Travel Air 4000	103	Mitsubishi A6M Zero
70	Travel Air 6000A	104	BAC 167 Strikemaster
71	Waco UPF-7	105	L-29
72	Breezy	106	Lockheed C-18 Lodestar
73	Waco YMF-5	107	Lockheed L-749 Connie
74	Interstate Cadet	108	Lockheed L-1049
75	Arctic Tern	109	DH 125
76	Marchetti 260D	110	Lockheed EC-121
77	Lockheed LASA 60	111	Lockheed L-1011
78	Islander (twin)	112	Douglas DC-3
79	Helio Stallion Dave Maytag's	113	Douglas DC-4
80	Helio 295 G0-480 turbo charged	114	Douglas A-26
81	Helio with round Russian engine	115	Curtiss C-46
82	Pilatus Porter Piston	116	Martin 404
83	Pilatus Porter Turbine Astazou	117	North American T-6
84	Pilatus Porter Turbine PT-6	118	North American SNJ
85	Cessna Caravan Soloy	119	North American T-28A
	Dual Pack PT-6 turbines	120	North American T-28B
86	Van's RV-3	121	North American B-25

122	North American P-51	CV-LB30 (B-24)
123	Consolidated PBY	CV-PBY5 (Catalina)
124	Bird Innovator PBY 4 engine	C-46
125	Argosy 4 engine RR turboprop	DC-3
126	LearJet	DC-4
127	Eagle XL Ultralight	Douglas B-26
128	Falcon 50	F-27
129	Ford Tri-Motor	L-1011
130	Lockheed Lodestar C-18	L-1049
		N-B-25

Helicopters

131	Hiller 12A	B-29
132	Hiller 12B	P-38
133	Hiller 12C	MI-A6M (Zero)
134	Hiller 12E	P-51
135	Hiller 12E4	T-28
136	Hiller FH 1100	G-TBM
137	Bell 206 Jet Ranger	
138	Bell Long Ranger Soloy Dual Pack	Helicopter—All makes and models single- and multiengine piston powered
139	Sikorsky S-58 turbine conversion	
140	Bell 47D-1	
141	Bell 47G-2	*Merrill also flew the C-119 and the*
142	Bell 47G-3B1	*Grumman SA-16 Albatross in the*
143	Robinson R-22	*Air Force and the Fairchild C-123*
144	Alouette	*in the Alaska Air National Guard.*
145	Enstrom	
146	Piasecki H-21	

Noel Merrill Wien Awards

Type ratings and LOAs

(Letters of Authorization) required to fly any airplane over 12,500 pounds gross weight, held by Merrill Wien

- The FAA's Wright Brothers "Master Pilot" Award

- The Alaska Aviation Community's Aviation Legend Honoree (2014)

Boeing B-17
Boeing 737
Boeing 727

- The Air Force Outstanding Unit Award

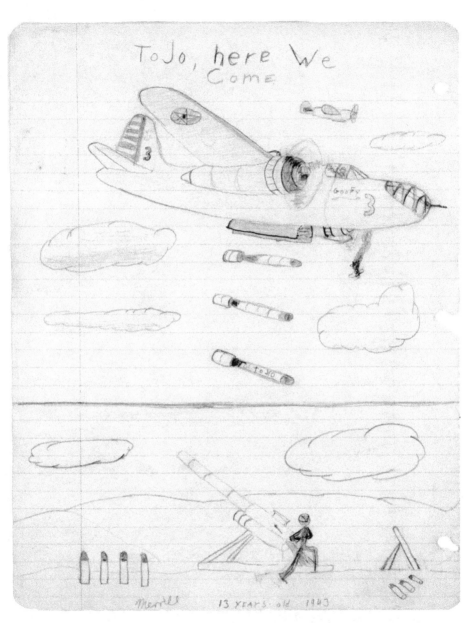

My rendering of a Douglas A-20 bomber, done at age thirteen during World War II. Drawings like this were posted in store windows to help sell war bonds.

Printed in the USA
CPSIA information can be obtained
at www.ICGtesting.com
JSHW012028140824
68134JS00033B/2935